MANAGING
EXPECTATIONS

Also Available from DORSET HOUSE

Complete Systems Analysis: The Workbook, the Textbook, the Answers
by James & Suzanne Robertson   foreword by Tom DeMarco
ISBN: 0-932633-50-1   Copyright ©1998,1994   624 pages, softcover

Creating a Software Engineering Culture
by Karl E. Wiegers
ISBN: 0-932633-33-1   Copyright ©1996   384 pages, hardcover

Exploring Requirements: Quality Before Design
by Donald C. Gause and Gerald M. Weinberg
ISBN: 0-932633-13-7   Copyright ©1989   320 pages, hardcover

Peopleware: Productive Projects and Teams, 2nd ed.
by Tom DeMarco and Timothy Lister
ISBN: 0-932633-43-9   Copyright ©1999   264 pages, softcover

The Psychology of Computer Programming: Silver Anniversary Edition
by Gerald M. Weinberg
ISBN: 0-932633-42-0   Copyright ©1998,1971   360 pages, softcover

Quality Software Management Series   by Gerald M. Weinberg

> **Vol. 1: Systems Thinking**
> ISBN: 0-932633-22-6   Copyright ©1992   336 pages, hardcover

> **Vol. 2: First-Order Measurement**
> ISBN: 0-932633-24-2   Copyright ©1993   360 pages, hardcover

> **Vol. 3: Congruent Action**
> ISBN: 0-932633-28-5   Copyright ©1994   328 pages, hardcover

> **Vol. 4: Anticipating Change**
> ISBN: 0-932633-32-3   Copyright ©1997   504 pages, hardcover

The Secrets of Consulting:
A Guide to Giving and Getting Advice Successfully
by Gerald M. Weinberg
ISBN: 0-932633-01-3   Copyright ©1988   248 pages, softcover

Surviving the Top Ten Challenges of Software Testing:
A People-Oriented Approach
by William E. Perry and Randall W. Rice
ISBN: 0-932633-38-2   Copyright ©1997   216 pages, softcover

Find Out More about These and Other DH Books:
Contact us to request a Book & Video Catalog and a free issue of *The Dorset House Quarterly,* or to confirm price and shipping information.

DORSET HOUSE PUBLISHING CO., INC.
353 West 12th Street   New York, NY 10014   USA
1-800-DH-BOOKS   (1-800-342-6657)   212-620-4053   fax: 212-727-1044
dhpubco@aol.com   http://www.dorsethouse.com

MANAGING
EXPECTATIONS

Naomi Karten

DH

DORSET HOUSE PUBLISHING
353 West 12th Street, New York, New York 10014

Library of Congress Cataloging-in-Publication Data

Karten, Naomi.
   Managing expectations : working with people who want
more, better, faster, sooner, now! / Naomi Karten ; foreword
by Gerald M. Weinberg.
         p.   cm.
   Includes bibliographical references and index.
   ISBN 0-932633-27-7
   1. Software engineering--Management.   2. Consumer
satisfaction.
   I. Title.
QA76.758.K37   1994
004' .068'4--dc20   93-48270
                                                        CIP

Text and Cover Illustrator: Conrad Cooper
Cover Design: Jeff Faville, Faville Design

Distributed in the English language in Singapore, the Philippines,
and southeast Asia by Toppan Co., Ltd., Singapore; and in the
English language in Japan by Toppan Co., Ltd., Tokyo, Japan.

Printed in the United States of America

Library of Congress Catalog Number 93-48270

ISBN: 0-932633-27-7   12 11 10 9 8 7 6 5

Dedication

To my husband, Howard,
my partner in exploration.

Acknowledgments

Many clients have asked me, kiddingly, whether their experiences and problems would appear in this book. Absolutely, I told them, but I promised anonymity, and have changed their names to ensure that anonymity. I appreciate their trust in me, and their openness in sharing their concerns.

Jerry Weinberg was a constant source of support throughout my writing and rewriting of this book. Through his suggestions and advice, he has shown me a learning curve that I am greatly enjoying climbing.

Wendy Eakin and David McClintock at Dorset House have impressed me with their caring attitude and their amazing attention to detail. I used to resist having my writing critiqued; in working with them, I have come to welcome it. I appreciate them for making this effort a truly collaborative one.

December 1993   N.K.
Randolph, Massachusetts

Contents

Foreword

The information industry is growing up. After four decades of fascination with our high-tech toys, some people in the industry are beginning to realize that we are not in the toy business, but the service business. A few have even realized that playing with high-tech toys isn't the only way—or even the best way—to better service.

One of the earliest of those few visionaries is Naomi Karten, author of *Managing Expectations*. I was first attracted to her work many years ago because she saw so clearly that the information industry was stuck—unless it could find a way to be more responsive to its customers. For many years, the newsletter she wrote, *Managing End-User Computing*, was a monthly reminder, prodding us to look up from our toys from time to time and cast our eyes on our customers.

Now, how could an industry as large as the information industry get so far removed from its customers that it needed visionaries to propose a service orientation? As industries go, we are large, but we are new. In mature industries, the customers have evolved along with the industry itself, and know what to expect. When you set out to buy a car, you're quite sure it won't cost a hundred dollars, nor is it likely to drain your purse of a hundred thousand dollars. When you order a steak, you expect neither a hamburger nor a steer. When you board a train for Chattanooga, you're confident you won't wind up in Oshkosh.

In the information industry, it's different. In our short history, we've seen numerous cases of systems development in which a job estimated at ten thousand dollars wound up costing a hundred thousand dollars. We've asked for a two-page report on sales of steak and gotten a thousand pages on sales of everything from hamburgers to steers. We've set out to buy a personal organizer and gotten an esoteric spreadsheet.

Because of our short, checkered history, our customers have no historical expectations except, perhaps, that when you cross the threshold of your information department, you abandon all hope of getting what you really want. Or, if they have no direct experience with information systems, our customers pick up expectations from analogous businesses—but those don't apply either.

Our customers expect little from us, or expect the wrong things, and in this they're not disappointed. We thought that as our technical prowess grew, our customers would be happier, but they aren't. To match our increasing ability to produce excellent systems, we need to increase our ability to manage our customers' expectations. Naomi Karten's pioneering book teaches us how to do it. Before you play with your toys again, read it!

September 1993   Gerald M. Weinberg
Albuquerque, New Mexico

Preface

I'm a student of human behavior and a dabbler in the art of managing expectations. It was not part of my master plan to become either the student or the dabbler. In fact, I was destined for greatness in the field of mathematics, and would, I'm sure, have achieved that greatness, were it not for day one of my class in linear algebra as a college freshman.

There, perched on a platform where she towered over a sea of mathematician wannabes, stood the most terrifying woman I had ever seen. She looked tough, and sounded even tougher. She was wearing high-heeled boots, and I, a member of the sneaker set, found this image frightening. In one of those memorable moments that shapes lives, I listened to this woman bellow at us, "If you don't learn the eighteen-step proof that A times one equals A, don't expect to pass this course!"

That, although I didn't know it at the time, was the beginning of my interest in the subject of expectations.

It was also the end of my not-yet-budding career in mathematics. I was into efficiency, and eighteen steps to prove A times one equals A was seventeen too many. A times one *did* equal A. What else *could* it equal?

I switched my major to psychology. I learned about motiva-

tion, learning theory, patterns of reinforcement, expectations
. . . . Well, there wasn't really a course in expectations, but
that's what many of the courses were about, as I realize in
looking back.

After getting a couple of degrees in psychology, I switched
focus again and became a programmer. That wasn't part of my
master plan either, but my husband, Howard, was a programmer, and he and his techie friends spoke a language I couldn't
understand. It was full of buzzwords, jargon, acronyms. I
couldn't stand not understanding that language, and decided
to become a programmer just for a short while, until I learned
some jargon.

To my great surprise, I got hooked. I discovered I loved
programming. I loved debugging. I loved the buzzwords, the
jargon, and the acronyms. And I loved working with our internal customers. Well, most of them, anyway. And even then, not
all day every day. They all seemed to have so many expectations. Occasionally, I found myself thinking, If it weren't for
the customers, this job could be fun.

I rose through several technical and customer support positions, and suddenly one day I was an information systems
manager. This, too, was not part of my master plan, but there
was a reorganization, and the next thing I knew, I was a manager. And before I could adjust my new chair so that my feet
could reach the floor, customers started calling, wanting to
know where their output was. They didn't care that I had just
started as manager an hour earlier, and they didn't want to
hear that the system had crashed, and that we were scrambling
to figure out why. All they knew was their output was due at
eight o'clock, and it was now nine o'clock. From that moment
on, almost every problem I experienced, witnessed, or heard
about revolved in some way or other around expectations.

I've now spent more than a decade as a speaker, seminar
leader, and consultant, and I've listened to countless stories
information systems professionals have told me about their
customers' misguided or hard-to-manage expectations.
However, what has become apparent from these stories is that
only rarely do these people see themselves as responsible for

the problems they face. Instead, in the vast majority of experiences, information systems personnel fault their customers for having unreasonable or unrealistic expectations.

Ironically, as I've listened to information systems customers describe *their* experiences, it has become apparent that systems professionals often have expectations of their customers that are just as unreasonable. In fact, it's intriguing how often systems professionals and customers accuse each other of exactly the same faults: withholding information, not listening, making false assumptions, and failing to understand their perspective.

My conclusion is that if each party sees the other as the problem, then the problem must belong to both. It is probable that we service providers bear responsibility for some of our customers' expectations. We may have done things, or failed to do things, that led our customers to have the expectations they have. And what about all those situations in which expectations on both sides have been perfectly reasonable, but different—only we didn't realize it until it was too late, because we mistakenly believed we understood each other, were talking the same language, and were striving for the same goals?

Despite all the factors that make customer/provider relationships difficult, such interactions should be win-win relationships, and can be if expectations are clarified early on. It is my hope that this book will help you gain a better understanding of the role expectations play in your relationships with those you serve, support, or interact with in the course of your work.

I hope it meets your expectations.

November 1993   N.K.
Randolph, Massachusetts

MANAGING
EXPECTATIONS

Introduction:
The Expectations Challenge

Managing expectations in today's turbulent business world is indeed a challenge, and it's not hard to understand why: Expectations affect a range of interactions with customers, including service responsiveness, service capability, product functionality, and project success. These types of expectations vary from one person to another, one situation to another, and one day to another.

Expectations are influenced by so many factors, such as lifelong beliefs, past experience, common sense, wishful thinking, false assumptions, external pressures, the wisdom of those we trust, and the slickness of those who mislead us. Expectations are further influenced by departmental and organizational priorities, management styles, and modes of operation. Expectations are likely to vary greatly across organizational and functional boundaries; the greater the number of business units involved in any given effort, the more expectations we must wrestle with at any one time. Furthermore, organizational cutbacks, competitive pressures, and technological change create even more expectations.

Given all these factors, the amazing thing about managing expectations is not how poorly we do, but how well.

1

THE EXPECTATIONS-MANAGING FRAMEWORK

In my work with organizations, I have been struck by the extent to which many problems revolve around three issues: communication (how to communicate with customers to create appropriate expectations); information gathering (how to determine customers' needs and evaluate solutions); and policies and practices (how to establish formal policies and sound practices to provide an infrastructure for managing expectations). Most problems in managing expectations can be eliminated or reduced with attention to these three issues. This book devotes a section to each of these issues, and each section contains four chapters that present related guidelines. The sections are described below.

Communication. The starting point for managing expectations is to become more conscientious about what you communicate and how. In both verbal and written communication, you may inadvertently contradict the messages you intend to communicate, without knowing you've done so. Problems in supporting customers crop up that don't make sense relative to what you think you communicated.

Guidelines 1 through 4 help you guard against conflicting messages, use jargon with care, identify communication preferences, and listen persuasively.

Information Gathering. The importance of information-gathering skills in managing expectations is simply stated: You can't meet customers' expectations if you don't know what they want. Yet, finding out is rarely straightforward; you can't just ask them and then assume they've told you what you need to know. In fact, it's safest to assume they haven't, because what they say they need may differ from what they actually need. And you must make very certain that your expectations are as reasonable and realistic as you want theirs to be.

Guidelines 5 through 8 describe how you can help customers describe their needs, become an information-gathering skeptic, understand your customers' context, and try the solution on for size.

Policies and Practices. Communication and information-gathering know-how will help you manage expectations on a case-by-case basis. However, in an organizational setting, something more is needed: an infrastructure that facilitates managing expectations consistently and over the long term. This third section concerns the policies and practices that clarify customer perceptions of your services, establish service standards, create reasonable boundaries on your workload, and most important of all, build strong relationships with customers. These policies and practices will help you and your customers create a shared understanding of what you can each expect from the other.

Guidelines 9 through 12 enable you to clarify customer perceptions, set uncertainty-managing service standards, say whoa (when appropriate), and build win-win relationships.

INVOLVING CUSTOMERS

Since a shared understanding is so central to the successful management of expectations, it makes sense that the very process of addressing this subject is something that can be shared. Therefore, as you begin to give it your attention, it is worthwhile to inform your customers that expectations management is a subject you are now paying more attention to, and to discuss how you and they can jointly improve your ability to work together. In fact, just raising and discussing the subject with your customers can improve your ability to meet each other's expectations.

For example, I've seen exciting results in systems-sponsored discussions on expectations-related issues. Two important aspects of the relationship with customers emerge in these discussions: first, the extent to which service providers and their customers already share similar views; and second, the extent to which service providers misjudge what is important to their customers.

Two such discussions stand out. In one, a specially scheduled session on success and risk factors in computing, systems personnel had expected their customers to dispute the necessity of following standards. They were surprised to discover the similarity between their own views and their customers'—not only about the factors that cause computer projects to fail, but also the standards that would improve the odds of success. Discovering the extent of their shared views was a major eye-opener for information systems staff that led to more open dialogue with their customers thereafter.

In another company, systems staff were surprised by how strongly their customers wanted not instantaneous service, as was expected, but simply to be kept informed on a timely basis.

For many participants, specially arranged forums of this kind provide the first opportunity they've ever had to discuss their concerns in a non-project-specific setting. And when differences in perspective arise—as they invariably do—participants have an opportunity to air these perspectives and exchange their views.

When systems professionals and their customers compare their views, they find a common ground that neither knew existed. In organizations that least expected it, I have even heard customers defend the reasoning of the systems organization to their own peers.

FORMULATING AN ACTION PLAN

You can make considerable headway in managing expectations by taking action on the twelve guidelines in this book, one by one, a little at a time, with one group of customers or another. Moreover, these guidelines provide a foundation on which to formulate a comprehensive expectations-managing action plan. Such a plan can help you systematically manage expectations—not just for the next customer, the next week, the next project, or the next interaction, but consistently and over the long term.

The concluding chapter of this book will help you translate your ideas into immediate action. One element of this plan entails something you may never have considered before: appointing someone to take primary responsibility for managing expectations. An expectations manager, in other words. More than a customer service representative, this person would implement the plan for your department or division and oversee efforts from an expectations-managing perspective. The concluding chapter describes the role and responsibilities of an expectations manager, and helps you assess whether such a role would be of value to your organization.

GETTING STARTED

To be able to quickly recognize useful strategies and techniques as you review the twelve guidelines in this book, start by identifying some specific expectations-related problems you'd like to resolve. The following three steps can help you pinpoint problems or situations you'd like to keep in mind as you read.

Step 1. Think about your current service strategies. In particular, consider these questions:

- How would you describe the overall level of customer satisfaction with your services?

- In your own view, are you delivering services effectively? As measured how?

- What are the biggest obstacles you face in successfully meeting customers' needs?

- What actions have you taken to eliminate these obstacles?

- What services would you like to change, and in what ways?

- How well do you believe you understand your customers' expectations?

- In what ways do you typically communicate with customers?

Evaluate your responses in terms of what they suggest about your service strategies, and make a mental note of the problems and concerns that came to mind as you responded. If possible, compare your coworkers' responses with yours. Major differences in responses among members of the same group may point to some problems in managing each other's expectations.

Step 2. Perform an expectations analysis. First, list some of the ways in which you're doing a good job in managing expectations. Second, list some of the ways in which you're doing a not-quite-so-good job. The second list often proves to be longer than the first, but be sure to give yourself credit for the things you're doing well. The very process of identifying what's working and what's not provides a context, as you read this book, for identifying opportunities for improvement.

Step 3. Target one or two key problems. Based on your assessment of your current service strategies, and the results of your expectations analysis, identify the key problems that you'd like to address. You may have many more than two such problems, but each one that you solve will ease the way for those that follow, so there's no need to try to solve all of them at one time. Chances are, you haven't previously analyzed problems in terms of expectations, so even if you select problems you've worked on before, you can now look at them from a new perspective.

TAKING THE CHALLENGE

In this age of corporate reorganization, and at a time when technology is becoming more complex even as it's becoming more useful, some people find it hard to believe that tackling an issue like expectations can make a difference. Yet it's precisely because of this organizational turbulence and technological complexity that it *can* make a difference, because managing expectations is a people issue—not an issue of products, tools, or methodologies. Given the current rate of change, focusing on people may be more important now than ever.

The challenge is yours to make expectations something you and your customers think about, discuss, and work together to resolve. Becoming better at managing expectations doesn't require an advanced degree, a multi-volume methodology, or a newfangled technology. It also doesn't require support from the top, a bottomless budget, or all the time in the world.

It's something you can do, starting immediately.

Section 1
Communication

The starting point for managing expectations is to become more conscientious about what you communicate and how. In both verbal and written communication, you may inadvertently contradict the messages you intend to communicate, without knowing you've done so. Problems in supporting customers crop up that don't make sense relative to what you think you communicated.

Guidelines 1 through 4 help you

1. Guard against conflicting messages.

2. Use jargon with care.

3. Identify communication preferences.

4. Listen persuasively.

1

Guard Against Conflicting Messages

How to avoid creating unintended expectations

One of the most concise conflicting messages I've ever seen is this juxtaposition of two signs on a country road in Vermont:

I have no idea how town authorities expect drivers to respond to these signs, but given my impatience at driving any slower than I have to, I decided the faster speed limit takes precedence.

Some situations, such as the juxtaposition of these signs, present a true contradiction. Other situations create only apparent contradictions. For example, near my office is a stretch of highway that has confused many travellers by simultaneously being labeled Route 128 south and Route 93 north. Unless you're going the other way. Then it's Route 128 north and Route 93 south. It seems like a contradiction until you realize that the only way a road can run north and south at the same time is if it's heading due east and west. Which it is.

COMMUNICATING CONFLICT

You can avoid being confused by a conflicting message by focusing on one of the choices and ignoring any other: In this case, focus on either the Route 93 sign or the Route 128 sign. Unfortunately, when conflicting messages occur in serving customers, the interpretation customers select may not be the one you prefer. This chapter describes six ways in which you may be communicating conflicting messages to your customers, and ways to avoid doing so.

Conflict #1: What You Promise vs. What You Do

Service-level commitments are a breeding ground for conflicting messages. For example, you can create a conflicting message if you lead customers to expect a level of service that differs from what you normally provide.

Promising What You Can't Deliver

Overeagerness to be responsive or the need to match or exceed the level of service provided by competitors may cause you to commit to an overly ambitious level of service. Companies that promise services within a specified period of time risk this type of conflict if they are unable to deliver on their promises.

Customers who fail to receive the promised services within the specified time period quickly learn to ignore the company's claims about its services and to expect, instead, the level of service actually delivered.

This conflict can also occur as the result of a well-intentioned plan to improve responsiveness. The plan may sound perfectly reasonable in theory, but may prove to be less so in practice. For example, to boost customer satisfaction, the manager of a customer service department established a new internal standard whereby all calls would be answered by the end of the second ring. Unfortunately, the number of calls far exceeded the ability of the staff to meet this standard. Staff members did the best they could, but soon found themselves answering the phone, shouting "I can't help you now. Call back later," and slamming the phone down in time to answer the next call. They met management's expectations; customers, meanwhile, quickly became disgusted with the service provided, and took their business elsewhere. From time to time, ask yourself what unreasonable expectations your own plans might create that would lead to a similarly conflicting situation.

Delivering More Than You Promise

A conflict can also occur if you promise a level of service, and then exceed it. This is certainly less serious than the previous situation, but it too can create unintended expectations. I realized this when I used to write a bi-monthly column which I routinely turned in to my publisher a week early. As one deadline approached, I completed my column two days later than usual, and my publisher called to find out where it was. In my eyes, I was still five days early, but in his eyes, I was two days late. Unknown to me, he had been basing his schedule on my normal delivery, not my formal due date.

Similarly, if you consistently complete projects for your customers before the date promised or deliver more than you promised, they will quite reasonably begin to expect results based on your performance history, not your promises. If you subsequently complete a project on the specified date, or deliver only what you agreed to, customers may be dissatisfied because you have no longer met their expectations, even though you did exactly what you said you'd do. The solution is certainly not to withhold all results that exceed expectations; simply be sensitive to the potential impact of doing better than customers expect.

Saying One Thing and Doing Something Else

A variation of this conflicting message is a discrepancy between what customers understand you to be saying and what they view you as doing. For example, while touting their role in helping customers achieve greater productivity, systems groups sometimes mandate software upgrades that necessitate considerable learning time and cause a temporary decrease in productivity. To many customers, this situation constitutes a conflicting message. This was the view of a corporate executive who said he didn't understand why he couldn't just be left alone to use the software he already had. The reasons for the upgrade may have been sound, but to customers unaware of these reasons, the imposed upgrade appeared to conflict with the goal of the people who mandated it.

Conflict #2: What You Say You Won't Do vs. What You Do

The previous category of conflicting messages concerns a conflict between what you say you will do and what you actually do. This second category is just the reverse: a conflict between what you say you *won't* do and what you actually do.

Servicing Non-Supported Applications

I've encountered such conflicts repeatedly in companies in which a systems group tells customers they don't or won't deliver a certain type of service, and then do so, anyway. For example, IS groups sometimes communicate this type of conflicting message when customers choose to develop their own applications, rather than to seek the support of the systems group. According to several IS managers, customer-developed applications are the customer's responsibility; the customer owns the application, and is responsible for any problems that subsequently arise.

But what actually happens when a problem arises? "They call us and we fix it," says one manager, whose response reflected that of peers in many companies. Personnel in many such IS organizations complain about continued customer reliance on them, while readily accepting ownership of the problem whenever the customer, temporarily, doesn't want it.

Servicing Non-Supported Products

Similarly, PC support groups sometimes communicate this type of conflicting message when they establish product standards. Policy manuals in countless organizations clearly state that customers can use non-supported products, but that any problems that result are their own responsibility. Nevertheless, when customers who use non-supported products call for help, support staff often provide assistance anyway. Usually, they have good reasons for doing so, such as the seniority of the customer, the urgency of the need, or the ease of quickly resolving the problem. But every time such assistance is provided, it further reinforces the expectation that help is available for the asking. Thus, although support staff members complain about the constant demands being made of them, they are often the cause of their own problem.

Systems personnel can be unaware of the impact of such support on customer expectations. This lack of awareness was typified by a PC specialist who complained to me about a customer whose disk crashed and who, despite repeated warnings, hadn't created a backup. The customer called, frantic. Despite explicit standards that only customers who had created backups would be eligible for recovery assistance, the PC specialist recovered the data. A few weeks later, when the customer again lost data and didn't have a backup, the PC specialist again provided immediate assistance. After the third such episode, the puzzled PC specialist asked, "Why don't they ever learn?"

The answer: They do learn. They learn there's no need to follow standards, because every time there's a problem, they can expect immediate help. This PC specialist had unknowingly become a master at creating conflicting messages.

Conflict #3: What You Imply vs. What You Do

Even without making an overt promise of service, it's easy to create a conflicting message. This was my conclusion after staying at a hotel in which the service was well below the usual standard for this hotel chain. After my visit, I received a customer satisfaction survey from hotel headquarters. One item asked if I had any complaints about my stay. I listed my complaints and offered some suggestions based on the way other hotels in the same chain had assisted me with similar situations.

Another survey item asked: "Would you like to be contacted about the problem you reported?" I checked yes.

Expecting a Follow-Up Response

This question led me to expect a phone call from hotel management in the near future. I was impressed by this service orientation; receiving such a call would have made me willing to forgive the hotel for a lapse in service. However, as of today, long after the incident, no one from the hotel has contacted me. And because the hotel created an expectation that has not been met, I now feel more disappointed by this hotel than if I had not been promised (as I perceived it) that I'd soon be contacted.

Expecting a Report of Results

Your customers may experience a reaction similar to mine when you request their feedback. Many customer surveys, for example, tell customers their feedback is important. As a result, some customers conclude that they will be informed about the results of the survey or changes that will be made as a consequence of those results. Such notification rarely happens, however. In fact, rarely do customers ever hear another word about the survey. The result is that even if changes are implemented as a consequence of the survey, customers see little connection between their own feedback and any changes made; some subsequently conclude their feedback is not so important, after all.

Customer surveys rarely say explicitly that customers will be provided with information about survey findings; any such assumption by customers is an inference only. However, this failure to follow up on what customers may perceive as a promise may be one reason that some organizations experience lower and lower response rates in subsequent surveys.

Conflict #4: What You Say vs. How You Say It

Conflict sometimes occurs between statements you make and the way you look or sound when you make them.

Speaking Face to Face

When I returned a rented car recently, the service representative asked, "How was the car?"

A thoughtful question, right? Possibly, but because of my interest in how organizations can improve their customer service, I was struck by the contrast between what this service representative asked and her demeanor and tone of voice in asking the question. The rote way she spoke, her glum expression, and the way she looked down at her terminal all suggested that she didn't really care about my response. She sounded as if she had been instructed to ask customers how they liked the car, without being advised that sounding uninterested undermined the value of the words.

When such conflicting messages occur, people are likely to give greater credence to the way you look and sound than to the specific words you use. It's often subtleties such as these that make the difference in how customers rate their satisfaction with the service they receive. And when customers have a choice of service providers, these small details can influence where they take their business.

Speaking of the Impossible

When I was a senior programmer analyst, I was assigned to a project team responsible for maintaining a series of systems that could win the gold medal in the Spaghetti Code Olympics. The systems had been malfunctioning regularly, and at my first team meeting, the project manager opened the meeting by saying, "I'm really depressed." Though she went on to assure us we were up to the task and could fix the problem, I doubt she realized the impact her opening comment had on the team. After all, a firm belief that we could do the impossible was essential to our doing so. She never exactly said she thought we would fail, but her demeanor made clear that she found the situation hopeless.

As it turns out, we did fix the problem, but not until this project manager was transferred because of "morale problems."

Speaking on the Telephone

On the phone, the message conveyed by your tone of voice is likely to overpower the message communicated by your words. Therefore, if you answer the phone sounding fatigued or bored, or revealing the stress you may be experiencing, callers can usually hear how you feel, even if your words suggest otherwise, and they may infer that you consider them an interruption or a nuisance. They can hear this message as clearly as if you said so explicitly, and it influences both their perception of you and how they feel you perceive them. As author Ralph Wilson points out, this situation can lead to a vicious circle: Callers react negatively to the negative tone of your voice and the resulting stress affects both parties.[1] Conversely, if you answer the phone sounding enthusiastic, you communicate to callers that you're pleased to hear from them. This is especially important in customer support. To the person with the problem, nothing is as reassuring as someone who sounds eager to help.

Speaking with a Smile

If you want to improve your telephone skills, listen to the way people answer your phone calls, and think about the impression they make on you. Identify the differences between those who sound pleased to talk to you and those who make you feel like an interruption. Then pay attention to your own voice on the phone, and particularly to the way you answer the phone. Have coworkers critique your telephone style.

Also, listen to radio commentators. When they smile while talking, you can actually hear that smile. Some customer service centers place mirrors near the phones so service representatives can see themselves smiling while on the phone. If being face to face with yourself all day isn't your style, post reminders that help you to think about how you sound.

Conflict #5: What You Write vs. What You Mean

Conflict can occur between the importance of information and where and how it is presented in written form.

Burying Policy

Important information can lose its prominence in written form if it gets buried in a document, as is often the case in policy manuals and service guides. For example, in one company's policy manual, a section on system security warns that a violation of security provisions may result in disciplinary action and possibly dismissal. Yet, this statement appears in a section that also includes information on course options and password formats, with nothing to distinguish this potentially career-ending statement from the rest. The way this message is presented conceals its importance, and could lead customers to miss it—or dismiss it.

Burying Notices

It's a common error to assume that, just because you've put something in writing, it has reached the intended party and will have the intended effect. For example, a systems analyst complained to me that although he had sent out an electronic mail notice corporate-wide to advise customers of an important change, many customers seemed to have remained unaware of it. The notice was important, but the way he communicated it told customers it wasn't—or more likely, didn't tell them anything, since it was buried among all the other messages in their electronic in-boxes. A brightly colored flyer may be an old-fashioned, low-tech solution, and may take a bit more work to prepare and distribute, but it's worth considering if getting customer attention is essential.

Setting critical information apart, highlighting it, or giving it an attention-getting look would help customers distinguish it from other information; otherwise, it may be unreasonable to assume that customers have seen the information, and even more unreasonable to think they will respond appropriately.

Conflict #6: What You Say vs. What Else You Communicate

Another category of conflicting messages is that in which the same party deliberately communicates messages with opposite meanings, yet both messages are valid. My husband, Howard, and I experienced just such a conflicting message when we went parasailing.

Mixing Risk with Benefit

Parasailing is an activity in which you spend ten minutes in midair, harnessed to a speedboat below and a parachute above.

"Is it safe?" I asked the attendant.

"Absolutely," he said, while handing us release forms to sign, to relieve him of responsibility for injuries incurred while we were up in the air being safe.

Observing that the landing was on a tiny raft out in the ocean, I asked if there were any chance of missing the raft and landing in the water.

"None," he said, while giving us life jackets to keep us from drowning if we landed in the water.

Messages that conflict by design serve different purposes. In the case of parasailing, the purposes might be viewed as marketing versus legal liability. Come-ons for "risky" activities focus on the thrill, the challenge, and the exhilaration, with no hint of possible danger. Then follows the warning about the potential downside. As an aficionada of conflicting messages, I collect release forms, and I'm intrigued by the lengths to which they go to describe the risks you can incur while having fun. One of my favorite warnings appeared on a ski lift ticket:

> Alpine skiing is a hazardous sport requiring deliberate and conscious control of your body through proper use of ski equipment in relation to ever-changing variables and dangers. Skiing safety is directly affected by your judgment in the severe elements of high mountain terrain. Ski only within your own ability. Be alert to continually changing weather, visibility, and surface conditions. Snow, ice, cliffs, rocks, roots, stumps, trees, debris, lift towers, ruts, bumps, snowmaking equipment, grooming vehicles, snowmobiles, other skiers, and a multitude of other objects are inherent to the sport of skiing. Be prepared to stop at all times. Never ski alone.

This warning, in type almost too small to read, is the first of two paragraphs on a ticket about three inches square. Perhaps the warning ought to simply say, *If you can't read this, stay home and be safe!*

Conrad '94

Moreover, perhaps there should be a release form for computing, modeled after the ski lift ticket, that would help create the right expectations:

> Computing is a hazardous activity requiring deliberate and conscious control of your operations through proper use of computer equipment in relation to ever-changing variables and dangers. Computing safety is directly affected by your judgment. . . .

CIRCUMVENTING THE CONFLICT

Conflicting messages serve as a reminder that everything you say and everything you do has the potential to influence perceptions and create expectations. Once you begin to think about conflicting messages, examples jump out at you everywhere, both in the work you do with customers and in situations when you are the customer. Continually ask yourself what expectations you may be creating that you'd prefer to avoid. Look especially for situations in which you violate your own standards. Think about how these conflicting messages might cause unreasonable expectations, and explore how you can eliminate the cause of the conflict.

Sometimes, you just have to find a clever way to circumvent the conflict. For example, an astute law-abiding driver might look at the 25 mph-35 mph speed limit signs and be relieved that, by driving twenty-five miles per hour or less, he'd be able to observe both speed limits at the same time. Voilà, no more conflict!

And if you're coming to visit me via Routes 93/128, just take the north/south route coming from the north or the south/north route coming from the south. I'll expect to hear from you when you call, in total confusion, from the east/west pay phone.

NOTES

[1]Ralph Wilson. *Help! The Art of Computer Technical Support* (Berkeley, Calif.: Peachpit Press, 1991), p. 81.

2

Use Jargon with Care
Speak to your listener's level

A few years ago, I went to a doctor I hadn't seen before. He marched into the examining room in his white "I'm the doctor" coat, peered at his file folder, and said, "I've reviewed your records, and you appear to be unremarkable."

In my mind, I slugged him—and would have actually done so (verbally, at least), except that I felt too undignified sitting there in the hospital gown they make you wear so that you feel too undignified to slug the doctor. Instead, I thought about what he said.

Moments later, I realized that his use of seemingly everyday language really was medical jargon for "based on what I see in your records, you're in great condition." In other words, his "unremarkable" was equivalent to my "remarkable."

"Right you are," I told him, beaming.

In the workplace, language that means different things to different people can cause more serious problems than just create the urge to slug; it can cause flawed outcomes, if not outright failures, if you each presume you're speaking the same language and have the same understanding—and the same expectations—of what you're trying to accomplish. In this chapter, we explore ways to communicate more effectively with customers by eliminating terminology that can lead to confusion, misinterpretation, and other forms of problematic communication.

MISCOMMUNICATING WITH TECHNICAL TERMS

A common obstacle to communication on technical matters is the use of terminology that's not understood by one of the parties. Here we look at three types of trouble with technical terms.

Muddling Messages

Sometimes, technical terminology seems to be used with the deliberate intent to confuse customers. That was my conclusion when I saw a newspaper that advertised a sale on vacuum cleaners. One vacuum cleaner was described as having a "super-powerful 720W motor." Another had a "strong 5-amp motor." A third offered "3.2 peak hp."

If you fiddle around with electrical widgets, you know that you can convert watts into amps and that "hp" has something to do with how effectively horses can clean your carpet. But if not, how would you know which one of the three vacuum cleaners would best meet your needs?

Alienating Listeners

The language of the systems world is especially confusing. Systems professionals love jargon, buzzwords, and acronyms and use them profusely. To those who don't understand the jargon, this terminology is mystifying. And that's the problem: The people you're communicating with may not understand what you mean. You can't be sure you'll meet each other's expectations if your very words confuse, annoy, or intimidate. You may not have to completely avoid such terminology, but if a meeting of the minds with your customers is important to you, it's wise to adjust the use of such terminology to your customers' level of technical sophistication.

For some situations, though, completely avoiding such terminology is best. That was the conclusion reached by an IS director in planning a presentation to senior management to propose the purchase of some expensive hardware. These executives were savvy businessmen, but they feared computers. Aware of this fact, the IS director told them he was there to propose the purchase of three pieces of hardware. "Let's just call them X, Y, and Z," he told them, and drew three boxes on the whiteboard which he labeled X, Y, and Z. "Don't worry what these boxes are," he told them. "It doesn't matter. What matters is what they'll do for you."

If his presentation had concentrated on computer concepts, hardware features, and technical jargon, he might not only have alienated his listeners; he might also have discouraged them from wanting to hear any of his future proposals. Instead, he focused his justification on the business perspective of his audience; he described costs, benefits, and risks, as well as the impact on the company of both acquiring the hardware and failing to do so. In emphasizing not what the hardware would do, but how it would help the company accomplish some of its important goals, he left the presentation with the executives' go-ahead for the purchase.

Speaking Technobabble

Of course, it's easy to forget to minimize your use of technical terminology when using it is second nature for you or when it's part of your culture. Fortunately for customers, the tables started to turn in the 1980s, as personal computers proliferated ("proliferate" being a term systems personnel initially used to mean "Customers are getting PCs, and we don't like it."). Aided and abetted by their born-to-compute toddlers, business professionals became technically proficient. In the process, they learned the vocabulary.

Given these changes, I became curious about the way in which technological advances had affected the customer/IS relationship, and polled some IS managers on ways that their relationships with customers differed from the "good old days." A majority of those polled responded that the biggest difference was customer mastery of technical terminology and technical know-how. In addition, several managers were distressed by their customers' increased expectations. "In the good old days," according to one such manager, "when there was a production failure, and customers called to ask what the problem was, we told them it was a problem with, oh, the franistan—or whatever gibberish came to mind. The customer said 'Fine, let me know when it's fixed.' It was so easy back then," the manager bemoaned. "Now," he said, "it's all changed. Now, when there's a production failure, the customer wants to know precisely what the problem is, precisely what caused the problem, and precisely what we intend to do to resolve the problem." Talk about changed expectations! He looked disgruntled as he said, "We can't baffle them with technobabble any more."

Not all managers polled shared this perspective, however. In fact, some felt that their relationships with customers had become significantly better. In describing their relationships, these managers used words previously unknown in the customer/IS context, such as teamwork, partnership, and synergy. "We now share a common language with our customers," they said. "We can talk about computer problems in proper technical terms." For these managers, technological change had helped to turn adversarial relationships into ones characterized by common perspectives and shared experiences.

It might be reasonable to conclude that with the sharing of a common technobabble, communication problems have disappeared. That conclusion, however, would be incorrect. The fact that communication problems are still rampant—and that both systems personnel and their customers still complain that the other doesn't understand them—underscores the fact that technical jargon isn't the only cause of problematic communication. In fact, because unfamiliar jargon is easy to identify, it is one of the simplest forms of communication problems to correct.

MISCOMMUNICATING WITH FAMILIAR LANGUAGE

Other kinds of communication problems, however, are less apparent, because they are caused by language that is either familiar to everyone or easy to understand. The problem is that it's easy to miscommunicate in this way, and not even know it. Consider the following four causes of problematic communication.

Differing Definitions

A major cause of problematic communication is language which you and your customers both understand, but interpret differently. Since the earliest days of PCs, stories of terminology-induced misunderstanding by novice PC users have been popular. One of the most familiar stories concerns the novice who was asked to send a copy of his diskette to the support staff, and photocopied the diskette. We may chuckle about such misinterpretations, but they make complete sense from that individual's perspective. Such examples illustrate the importance of using even the most familiar words with care.

Similar to misinterpretations of phrases like "copy of the disk" are misinterpretations caused by terms that have precise, yet different, meanings in different parts of an organization. Often, it's the most familiar terms that can create the greatest confusion, not only between systems staff and their customers, but also between multiple customer areas. This makes a sensitivity to terminology even more important in efforts that span departmental or organizational boundaries.

Take the experience of two agencies of the federal government. Both agencies generated a report on imports of petroleum into the United States by month, but the figures in the two reports were completely different. When employees discovered the discrepancy and investigated it, they found they were defining petroleum differently, and were reporting on different categories of crude and refined petroleum. To make certain that this was indeed the cause of the discrepancy, they made some adjustments and reran the reports. The figures still differed. Then they found that their definitions of the United States differed: One agency defined it as the fifty states; the other included territories such as the Virgin Islands. Again, they made adjustments and reran the reports. The figures were closer, but still didn't match.

At first, it seemed impossible that the meaning of "month" could account for the discrepancy. After all, how could such a well-understood term have multiple definitions? But it did. One agency defined a month as a calendar month, while the other agency defined it as the period from the tenth of one month to the ninth of the next. They made additional adjustments and reran the reports. Did the figures match? As it was described to me, it was close enough for government work!

Situations in which definitions differ are far from unique. I once managed a system in which all months were treated as if they had thirty days. For us, thirty days hath September, April, June, . . . as well as all the rest of the months, and sometimes we actually forgot the world didn't really operate that way. In fact, it's the rare organization that doesn't have multiple definitions of month or other "obvious" terms, such as order, sale, and even customer. In fact, in some companies, no two departments agree on the number of customers the company has, because each counts customers differently.

In all these situations, none of the definitions is wrong. Each term has a precise definition that supports the needs of the specific area of the organization. It's for that very reason that these terms are jargon: They have specialized meanings that may make no sense out of context. Normally, problems don't arise until comparisons are made, or people attribute incorrect definitions to the terms, or systems operate on differently defined data as though they reflect common definitions.

As an IS project manager, I was repeatedly called into meetings to referee disputes between departments whose reports were supposed to be identical, but which, like those of the government agencies, didn't match. They each insisted their report was correct and the reports of the others were erroneous. More often than not, I found that all the reports were correct, but that each department stored, manipulated, and reported data differently to meet its specific business needs. Is this a systems problem? Not at all. But when apparent discrepancies such as this one occur, customers frequently assume it *is* a systems problem. Therefore, the discrepancy becomes your problem if customers expect you to diagnose and resolve it.

As such examples show, it pays to be on the lookout for potential sources of ambiguity. You can do this by taking the following steps:

• Incorporate definition-checking into your project methodologies, to remind yourself to double-check and clarify your understanding of your customers' terminology. Known instances of multiple definitions should be documented for use throughout the systems organization.

• Monitor your next several information-gathering sessions, and see if you can identify instances of terminology that could contribute to misunderstandings. Even better, next time you meet with customers, have a coworker track your terminology. You may be startled by how often you use familiar terminology that has one meaning to you and another to your customers.

• Educate customers to be sensitive to differences in definitions. For example, you can use meetings with customers to relate stories about actual or potential terminology mix-ups, with emphasis on mix-ups in your own organization, and invite customers to share their experiences. You can also use newsletters and other forms of written communication with customers to highlight terms you know to have multiple meanings.

• Ensure that in any endeavor involving multiple customer areas, adequate attention is given to issues of terminology that might have different meanings to different departments. There are more than enough definitions of month to go around!

Ambiguous Statements

A second cause of miscommunication is the use of terminology that has different meanings in different circumstances. For example, words such as "quickly" are particularly prone to creating inappropriate expectations if steps are not taken to eliminate any ambiguity. How quick, after all, is quickly?

Such words create expectations in customers that may differ from what you intended. For example, when you promise to return a call soon, could the caller think you mean one hour, when what you actually mean is a week from Tuesday? Similarly, when systems staff plan software upgrades, they often advise customers that the upgrade will help them do their work better. "Better for whom?" asked a corporate vice president I spoke to, who had learned from experience to equate what the systems staff called "better" with substantial lost time while he adapted to the better way.

Policy manuals and service guides are filled with ambiguous, imprecise language, such as the following statements taken from documents that organizations have sent me for review. I've added the italics.

- "Users should log off when they leave the office for *extended* periods." Meaning ten minutes or a day?

- "Change passwords on a *regular* basis." Once a day? Once a year?

- "Users will be given advance notice if possible before being *forced off* a system that must be brought down." A visit by the PC police, perhaps?

- "Users are asked to *exercise caution* in bringing in outside diskettes." By looking both ways before crossing?

Customers cannot be held responsible for failure to adhere to policies and standards they interpret differently from the way you intend. Before finalizing such documents, it's a good idea to review them carefully to determine if they might raise more questions than they answer—or worse, raise no questions at all, because customers "clearly" understand the information to mean something different from what you actually mean. In preparing such material, ask: Is this information precise? Will it lead customers to take the action we intend? How might customers misinterpret this information?

Ambiguous or unclear communication can also be the result of the absence of information rather than its presence. Policy documents and service guides often direct customers to take a particular action, without explaining why. Yet, explanations can help customers understand the relevance of the stated action and ensure they don't misinterpret it or view it as an arbitrary order. Statements such as the following might very well lead a customer to ask "Why?"

- "We encourage users to exchange documents electronically, rather than using fax machines."

- "Establish an audit trail to monitor when an application is accessed."

- "All requests for data downloading must be reviewed by Internal Audit."

In the material I've reviewed, explanations are most often lacking precisely for the directives that are the most important for customers to understand and follow. Yet, in the absence of an explanation, many customers simply ignore the information.

If you review your own documents with these concerns in mind, you will undoubtedly identify certain ambiguities that you might otherwise overlook, but the only way to be sure of doing a thorough review is to solicit customer feedback. Ask customers to identify words or statements that are unclear. Then ask how they would interpret certain statements, particularly those for which a specific action or understanding on their part is critical. If you distribute policy and service information to customers with no prior feedback from them, you relinquish the right to be mystified when they fail to heed your advice.

Misguided Labels

A third problem in communication is caused by everyday language that offends. The offensive language could be something as simple as the designations and labels you use, as I learned from one of my most memorable terminology-induced traumas as a manager.

I was managing the development of a major system for a team of customers who performed a financial function known by the acronym BOC. These customers were known as the BOC team. The system was also to be used by three smaller teams in the same department, whose tasks followed logic that was similar for the three but different from the BOC logic. The combined workload of these three teams was considerably less than that of the BOC team.

My staff designed a system that had two major components of logic. One was for BOC processing, and the other pertained to the three smaller teams, which we designated as NONBOC. When the system was completed and it was time for the grand presentation to our customers, we described the two components of the system, BOC and NONBOC.

As soon as we finished our presentation, a distressed NONBOC representative asked why we referred to the small teams in terms of what they weren't, rather than what they were.

It quickly became clear that to her, and to others from these three "lesser" areas of the department, this was no trivial matter. Having responsibility for tasks that were fewer in number, took longer to complete, and had a smaller financial impact, the members of these three teams undoubtedly had less clout in the department and were treated accordingly. They were understandably angry that our naming terminology further emphasized that situation.

Talk about making customers feel unremarkable! Clearly, we had blundered, not in our system design, but in our terminology. We had used the term NONBOC not just throughout the system, but also in our presentation to our customers and in the user manuals.

I learned that day to think more about how easy it is for innocently assigned designations to have negative consequences far out of proportion to the unintended slight. Even the most innocent language can trigger unintended consequences.

In an episode similar to that of the offensive naming standard, a help desk got into trouble because of the name it gave a report. Like many help desks, the staff regularly collected data regarding their customers' calls, and periodically summarized these statistics by department to produce reports for distribution to customer departments. They believed that such information would help customer management track problems and identify trends, but something as seemingly innocent as what they called the report made a big difference in how management perceived and used it. They called this particular report "Problem Report." It *was* a problem report, but it never occurred to staff members to consider how this might sound to the recipient managers.

One manager read it and interpreted it to mean that when he and his staff asked for help, they were a problem. He didn't like being perceived as a problem, so he advised his department that they were no longer to call the help desk. Henceforth, they would solve all technical problems themselves. In so doing, he propelled his department into a state of premature self-sufficiency.

Fortunately, most of the department's technical problems were easy to fix without outside help. However, when departmental staff members attempted to solve technically intricate problems, little problems turned into big ones. One such problem was traced to a broken chain in a database. Traced, that is, after staff members finally gave in and called the help desk, having already spent much longer attempting to fix the problem than they should have, turning an easily recoverable problem into a database nightmare.

Maybe it's nit-picking to make an issue of the wording of a report title, but I think not. Such seemingly trivial situations can color customers' perceptions, and can sometimes contribute much more to whether or not they feel you met their expectations than even on-time completion of the project.

What would have been good alternatives in these two situations? In the BOC situation, we might have created a prefix based on the initial letter of the three types of non-BOC processing, or found some other element in common to the three customer teams. Or, we might have asked the teams how they referred to themselves collectively. We might also have presented an overview of the system to our customers much earlier in the development cycle. That way, if they had a grievance, we'd know about it, and could make changes or at least discuss the problem and avoid future surprises.

What should the help desk report have been called? There are many possible titles that would focus on its positive aspects, such as "Support Report," to emphasize the service provided; or "Call Analysis Planning Guide," to suggest the use of the report to help identify staffing or training needs. It could even have been titled "Problem Resolution Report," to put the emphasis on something being fixed rather than something being broken. But the specific title is not as important as the support of customers for whatever title is used. As with the BOC report, a sample report could have been shown to customers, before going public, to get their reactions to it.

Some organizations have created formal mechanisms for gaining customer feedback, by establishing customer-based advisory boards or steering committees that serve as an ongoing point of contact for the systems group on designated issues. Such groups can be helpful in providing or arranging for feedback on material that will be widely disseminated, have corporate impact, or span organizational boundaries. Certain other individuals might be invited to offer their feedback, on a case-by-case basis; for instance, the manager who reacted negatively to the problem report would be a natural.

Code Words

Terminology intended strictly for private use can cause offense and damage customers' perceptions of you if it reaches them. For example, I once consulted with a technical support group that was plagued by repeat calls regarding what they viewed as simple problems. In describing this situation, they started referring to these calls as "silly calls." Initially, they meant that they considered the questions silly and the callers somewhat lacking in brainpower. However, as we discussed their service strategies, they concluded that they were part of the problem for not having done enough to eliminate the conditions that led customers to have such questions in the first place.

As we discussed service modifications that would reduce the volume of such calls, the phrase "silly calls" stuck. Its meaning changed to refer to the inadequacies in their own services, rather than the nature of the calls they received. However, it might have been preferable to squelch the phrase altogether, rather than run the risk of inadvertently using it in the presence of customers.

Beware of your own internal vocabulary. Every group has

its own set of code words, but you must be careful not to let code-word use become so natural that, like the silly calls, it could cause a misunderstanding.

MISINTERPRETING CUSTOMERS' LANGUAGE

The previous examples describe customers' misinterpretations of each other's terminology or yours. But just as they can misunderstand you, you can misunderstand them. One source of such misunderstanding is the customer-satisfaction survey. Systems groups that conduct such surveys typically interpret customers' responses in their own terms, rather than verifying what their customers actually meant.

In one systems division's survey, for example, customers rated division staff high on responsiveness, cooperation, and reliability, but much lower on consistency, adaptability, and innovativeness. Division personnel planned to follow up with customers to learn more about what contributed to their low ratings; however, they did not intend to seek similar information about what contributed to the high ratings. Staff members simply assumed that they and their customers interpreted terms like "responsive," "cooperative," and "reliable" identically.

Is this a safe assumption? The systems staff interpreted the high rating for responsiveness to mean that customers were pleased with their speed of response to requests. It's possible, though, that what customers actually meant was that they liked the department's flexibility in continually making last-minute modifications—modifications the staff didn't want to make and planned to refuse to make in the future. This misinterpretation could lead the group to focus unduly on their speed of response so as to ensure a continued high rating for responsiveness—and end up with a lower rating because they no longer made last-minute modifications.

The key to avoiding terminology-related misinterpretations of customers' expectations is to have customers clarify what these terms mean to them. In addition to asking customers for definitions, ask them for examples of things you've done that illustrate their impressions. These examples can be requested as part of the survey itself, or as part of follow-up interviews. By focusing on concrete examples that illustrate their interpretation of these terms, you can avoid the confusion caused by differing interpretations, and gain a better understanding of what you should change to meet their expectations.

JARGON-CHECKING KEPT IN PERSPECTIVE

Obviously, you can carry a good thing too far. You can analyze every word from every conceivable angle, until you're ready to lock yourself in a room for fear of having overlooked some subtle shading or unintended implication. The point is not to go to extremes, but simply to ask yourself how others might misinterpret your words or how you might have misinterpreted another's. Think about your own buzzwords and jargon, as well as those of your customers. Second-guess each other's use of any terminology that can befuddle. Be especially careful in the use of everyday, familiar, you-know-it-and-I-know-it terminology that sounds innocent, but might actually be anything but. Raise awareness about the sources of problematic communication, and the way words can mislead or confuse.

Remember, though, that raising this awareness may have its risks. In a keynote presentation on managing expectations, I used the experience of the doctor I nearly slugged as an example of how easy it is to offend or create confusion. When my presentation ended, the president of the organization came up to me, shook my hand, and said "That was unremarkable!" Hmmm. . . .

3

Identify
Communication Preferences

One method does not serve all

You can communicate goals, objectives, tasks, procedures, constraints, interdependencies, timetables, priorities, responsibilities, and accountabilities—and still not meet your customers' expectations. You can deliver a solution that perfectly addresses your customers' needs, and still not meet their expectations. Why? Because for some customers, *how* you communicate is more important than *what* you communicate. Such customers are concerned with *process,* that is, with how well your communication style respects and accommodates their communication preferences. For such customers, meeting their process expectations is even more important than meeting their project expectations.

What makes communication preferences especially difficult is that they vary not only from one customer to another, but also from one circumstance to another. A customer who wants a lot of information at one time may want very little at another. To complicate matters further, customers rarely tell you their communication preferences, making it your job to investigate. This guideline provides examples of different communication preferences, and describes some techniques for identifying and working with your customers' preferences.

COMMUNICATING STATUS INFORMATION

It took a major confrontation for me to appreciate the importance of communication preferences. It happened when I was an IS manager, and one of my responsibilities involved developing a complicated system for a division widely reputed as being hard to work with. The division manager was Charlie, who was demanding, unyielding, and resistant to views other than his own. "We've been burned by IS," he told us repeatedly, and it was clear he expected it to happen again. My staff and I were determined to prove him wrong.

The project would have been challenging even under friendlier circumstances: The scope of the system was vast and the logic intricate; the deadline was externally mandated and nonnegotiable. The four years of monthly files needed to initialize the system resided in dozens of departmental files—and departmental staff had named these files after cities, cars, and baseball teams! Documentation for these files consisted largely of handwritten notes. On top of all this, Charlie and his division hated us simply because we were IS. It was any manager's worst nightmare.

Despite obstacle after obstacle, however, my development team was on time and on target. I thought Charlie would be thrilled. He wasn't. I gave him weekly status reports describing our consistent progress. I assured him work was proceeding smoothly, and we were meeting our milestones. He rejected the reports and insinuated I was lying. He reminded me again that he'd been burned by IS.

Convinced that we weren't getting the job done, Charlie sent a steady stream of complaints about us to Nathan, his vice president. I notified Victor, my own vice president, about the situation. Initially, the vice presidents kept their distance, hoping we'd work things out on our own, but when the situation intensified, they decided to intervene. What we would all do, they decided, would be to spend an evening together to try to resolve our differences.[1]

The evening began with dinner. We sat on one side of the table and talked among ourselves. They sat on the opposite side and did the same. Fake smiles passed back and forth. Charlie talked baseball, revealing the names of several files in the process. We were civil to each other, but no one was fooling anyone.

After dinner, we regrouped in the executive conference room, where a table was set up in a large U shape. A fifteen-foot gap separated one side of the U from the other, and our customers, in unison, marched to one leg of the U and sat down. We did the same on the opposite side. And there we sat, staring across a canyon at each other.

Nathan's Preference

Our customers took the offensive, and with Nathan leading the attack, hurled complaints and accusations at us. Victor did his best to defend us, but these folks were angry. Logical responses such as "But we *are* on time" weren't going to work. Then, in one of those moments I'll remember forever, Nathan scowled at me, and, with the full weight of his voice on each word, said, "*I . . . think . . . you're . . . incompetent.*" I can hear it to this day.

Well, I'm not perfect, and I know it, but I prize competence above almost all else, and one thing I know positively is that

I'm not incompetent. We were getting the job done—but if this is how Nathan perceived things, then this, for him, was the truth.

Finally, Victor looked at Nathan and asked the question that changed the course of the evening: "What do you want?"

One long moment later, Nathan said, "I want a picture. All I want is a picture." It seemed unbelievable, but it was true. He wanted a graphical representation of our status reports.

Building a Skyscraper

Although Nathan's request initially seemed strange, it made sense. The building of a complex system, unlike the building of a skyscraper, is an intangible process. You can't pass by once a day, gaze at the construction, and watch it progress from a hole in the ground to a sixty-story edifice. When you develop a system, it may be a million lines of code, but it's still invisible. And things that are both invisible and technical are, to those who don't understand them, mysterious, elusive, threatening, and not to be trusted—and so, too, are the people who develop those invisible, technical things.

Up to that point, we'd given our customers both verbal and written status reports. We'd met each milestone in our project plan, but Nathan couldn't see the system, and neither could Charlie.

This was back when mammoth mainframes ruled the earth, and PC graphics were a thing of the future. Nevertheless, now knowing what Nathan wanted, we began to prepare status reports consisting of graphs, diagrams, and charts, with a paragraph describing each one. We presented a visual report to Nathan every two weeks. And he was, if not always happy, at least less distrustful. He still made me the occasional object of his target practice, but it was never with quite as much venom.

This single event did not turn a troublesome project into a team picnic, but it did help me realize that, to manage customers' expectations, you must do more than focus just on project deliverables, even when you're on time, under budget, and all is well with the world. You must also consider how you work with customers.

The idea of a visual representation may seem obvious now that you can produce the graph of your choice in minutes. Back then, though, chart-making was slow, plodding manual labor, and not a customary component of any reporting process. The fact that it could make a genuine difference in managing Nathan's expectations never occurred to me. This is not to say that the format of a status report is more important than its content; a visual report describing schedule slippages would not have spared us Nathan's wrath. However, neither did a non-visual report of our on-time status. Since a visual representation of our status was important to Nathan, that made it important to the success of this project.

COMMUNICATING IDEAS

With Nathan, the issue revolved around how we communicated status information. Different people may have other preferences that can determine their receptiveness to the information you send them.

These preferences often vary significantly from one person to another, as I learned from three of my IS superiors: Mike, Walter, and Bob. Mike, my director, liked paper, especially paper filled with charts. He thrived on spreadsheets, and giving him lots of paper filled with lots of spreadsheets improved the odds of getting his attention.

At another point in time, I worked for Walter, a division manager who like Mike was paper-happy. However, Walter was fond of words, not charts. He issued memos galore, and his incessant paperwork drove his employees crazy. With every reorganization, department managers held their breath, fearing they'd end up working for him.

By the time I came to work for him, I saw I'd have a better chance of succeeding with him if I accepted his communication preferences, and responded accordingly. One way I did this was by periodically preparing wordy reports for him. This strategy led him to feel that I understood him, and it caused him to go to bat for me more than for the other managers in his division. They could have accomplished the same just by sending him an occasional memo, but they failed to understand that I was successful in working with Walter, not despite his idiosyncrasies, but because of them.

The communication preferences of Bob, an assistant vice president who was Mike's superior, differed significantly from both Mike's and Walter's. Bob was a man of few words. He made decisions quickly and didn't want anything in writing. Gaining his attention meant talking, and doing so concisely. Managers accustomed to Mike's style, and oblivious to individual differences, mistakenly plied Bob with paperwork and excessive detail; when he ignored them, they failed to understand why peers who did no more than chat with Bob occasionally were more successful in getting his approval for their recommendations.

Be warned, however, not to become too accustomed to a communication style that works. One senior vice president, Dave, told me about an experience that almost ended his tenure as a senior VP. It was tough getting time to pitch ideas to his CEO, but they'd occasionally run into each other in the elevator. So Dave learned to package his ideas into snippets of thirty seconds. Then, whenever he saw the CEO in the elevator, he was prepared to take advantage of the opportunity. During the brief time in transit, Dave completed his proposal, and the CEO ruled on it.

When the CEO retired, Dave continued to treat his successor in the same way, and nearly got fired. Why? Because the new CEO didn't understand what was going on. Who was this fast talker, and why did he always expect an instant answer? Dave, for his part, was mystified as to why he no longer got a quick decision on his proposals. Fortunately, he realized just in time that the problem wasn't with his ideas, but his method of communicating them. This new CEO, unlike the previous one, needed to feel he had enough information before he made a decision. He wanted to discuss the issues, weigh the alternatives, and consider the tradeoffs—and he wanted to do it sitting down and face-to-face, not standing and on the run.

ACCOMMODATING DIFFERENCES IN PREFERENCES

It is not unusual for service personnel to view their customers as if they are a single homogeneous group, with identical styles, attitudes, and modes of operation. The fact is, though, that customers are usually as different from each other as they are from the people who serve and support them.

Think about the various departments in your organization: marketing, engineering, finance, human resources, and so on. Although striving toward common goals, each has its own priorities, pressures, time frames, and objectives. So, too, do the work groups within each department. Departments also vary in such things as the emphasis they place on speed, accuracy, cost, and flexibility. Furthermore, individuals within a single work group often exhibit major differences in such things as their attitude toward change, their ability to see the big picture, and their attention to detail.

Here's a list of five steps you can take toward discerning and accommodating your customers' preferences:

1. Be cognizant of your customers' communication styles. How would you characterize the departments you work with?

Consider such things as their pace of activity, receptiveness to new ideas, style of decision-making, adherence to protocol, preference for individual versus team efforts, and level of risk-taking.

2. Think about how you can modify your communication style to mesh with your customers'. For example, if you're working with a department that likes to take risks and learn by doing, it may not be wise to encourage too much analysis. Or, if a particular department's style is to be slow, plodding, and methodical, members of the department will be more likely to view you favorably if you accept their approach, and even encourage it, than if you rush them. By your standards, it may not feel like you're rushing them, but it's their perception that counts. Or, if a department makes decisions by consensus, you may need to communicate with several members of the department in order to sell your ideas or gain buy-in. By contrast, if they make decisions by fiat, you need to know who the chief decision-makers are, and adapt your approach accordingly.

3. Spend time with your coworkers analyzing differences between your customer areas. Identify the key characteristics of each, and think about how you can adapt your style to accommodate theirs. The better you can mirror the dynamics of your customers, the more comfortable they are likely to be with you.

4. Don't wait until customers complain to consider their preferences. Ask your customers to verify your own observations and analyses. Ask questions rather than take anything for granted. Build into your project methodology a way to determine communication preferences. Ask customers, for example, if they'd like status reports to focus on general information or details. Find out whether they want to be advised of every deviation from the project plan, or just those that exceed some prespecified limit. Inquire whether they want to be notified by telephone, electronic mail, paper document, fax, or in person. If you're preparing proposals or reports, ask customers whether they like quantitative or qualitative information, and whether they prefer charts, narrative description, or thirty-second briefs. Ask how they would characterize their department's

communication style and preferences, and the style and preferences of particular individuals with whom you'll be working.
Or offer your preferred approach, but give your customers a
chance to suggest alternatives.

**5. Remember that communication preferences may
change over time and over the course of a project.** For example, multi-color charts may suffice early in a project, but later
on, a narrative approach may be preferable. Or, you may have
customers who prefer to take their time making decisions, but
then will want quick action once that decision has been made.
Review your customer's preferences throughout the life of a
project, periodically asking if they're comfortable with the way
you're working together.

Many customers have never been offered choices on such matters, and some customers won't particularly care what
approach you use so long as you produce results. But everyone
cares, at least, about being asked. The fact that you show an
interest in their preferences may impress them and increase the
odds of your success in communicating with them, working
with them, and meeting their expectations.

GAINING CONSENSUS AND ACHIEVING BUY-IN

Few process issues are as crucial to whether customers perceive that you have met their expectations as buy-in: If they
judge that their views have been taken into account, they are
more likely to feel that you have met their expectations. For
many people, having an opportunity to express their views is
sufficient for them to feel they have a stake in the outcome.

In organizations, generating buy-in may require meeting
with the various parties to an effort and giving each an opportunity to present his or her views. Time-consuming though it
may be, soliciting these views is too important an activity to
bypass. However, as the number of participants and the number of customer areas involved in an effort increases, it
becomes increasingly difficult to generate consensus from their
different and perhaps strongly held views. If a consensus is

either necessary or desirable in making key decisions, then you face a challenge, because almost any decision is likely to win the support of some participants, and to be resisted and resented by others. In such circumstances, special methods are required.

A Technique for Building Consensus

One such method for gaining consensus is the Delphi process, a technique that can be especially effective when a decision must be reached on an issue that involves numerous different viewpoints. The process entails polling a group of individuals on an issue, having them privately prepare their responses, documenting the responses without listing names, and redistributing all of them to each individual. Participants are then polled again, and the process is repeated until the group has reached a strong consensus. Interestingly, achieving this consensus often takes no more than one or two iterations. This process allows participants to reassess their opinions in light of the views of others, and to change their opinion privately, without being pressured to do so, or embarrassed by doing so.

For example, a project manager named Sarah used a Delphi process to select the product that would best meet her organization's needs. She sensed that if she made the decision unilaterally, her customers would reject or resist her decision. After only two iterations, the group Sarah polled reached agreement about the product they wanted. It was the one Sarah would have selected herself, but now these representatives from throughout the organization "owned" the decision and felt a stake in the success of the product.

I asked Sarah whether she thought the product-selection team members would have reached agreement as quickly through discussion, and whether they would have reached a unanimous decision if they had communicated their views publicly. "Unlikely," she said, "because public discussions become too political. What made the difference was that participants were able to review other participants' responses. As a result, everyone was more receptive to compromise."

This type of consensus-building process has numerous benefits: It allows participants to communicate their opinions freely, and to change their views without losing face. It prevents embarrassment to those who know less than others, and gives those who might withhold their views a chance to participate. Most importantly, it enables people to make decisions objectively, without concern for political considerations. As a result, it brings closure to decisions that otherwise might be unsatisfactorily resolved.

LEARNING FROM PREFERENCES

The very process of communicating about preferences is one of the most important techniques you can use to manage expectations. Of course, finding out what customers expect of you doesn't mean you can necessarily meet those expectations. And clarifying what you expect of customers doesn't mean they'll comply. But by raising the issue and identifying differences in expectations, you are in a much better position to resolve problematic differences before they loom large.

After listening to me spout at length on this subject, my husband, Howard, is trying to learn how to generate my buy-in for his decisions. As the cook in the family, he recently asked me what time I expected dinner:

> Me: I expect dinner at seven o'clock.
>
> Him: Sorry, it won't be ready until seven-thirty.
>
> Me: Well, if you already knew that, why did you bother asking?
>
> Him: Because now you feel like you had a say in the decision before I go and do it my way.

He hasn't quite got the idea yet, but we're working on it.

NOTES

[1]What these vice presidents hoped to accomplish in our evening together was a greater sense of teamwork between our two organizations. DeMarco and Lister refer to the process of team formation as "jelling," and point out that when a team does come together, it's worth the cost, because the work is fun, and the people are energized. [See Tom DeMarco and Timothy Lister, *Peopleware* (New York: Dorset House Publishing, 1987), p. 156.] In this case, team formation earlier in the effort might have made a major difference in our subsequent ability to work together and to understand each other's expectations.

4

Listen Persuasively

When listeners listen, talkers talk

When I was a twelve-year-old at summer camp, two of my bunkmates disliked each other. One, I considered a friend; the other, I didn't care for. At the end of the summer, each girl came to me and thanked me for taking her side. This surprised me. I didn't recall spending much time listening to either of them, and certainly not to the one I disliked. Yet their appreciation showed me that people's perception that you are listening can lead them to feel comfortable with you and to open up to you. Years later, I realized that this experience marked the unofficial start of my consulting career.

This chapter's guideline is about how to improve two overlapping skills: listening and showing that you're listening. It may seem strange to refer to the latter as a skill, but it is; knowing how to show that you're listening can help you excel in your information-gathering and relationship-building efforts. When customers view you as interested in what they are saying, they feel more encouraged to respond to your questions, and to give you the information you need to fully understand their expectations. Even more important, though, is the reverse situation: If you do not appear to be listening, you might unintentionally discourage customers from elaborating on their needs. The result is two-fold: You risk depriving yourself of important information, and you risk creating a negative perception of your services.

APPEARING NOT TO LISTEN

You can be listening to your customers intently, but if it's their impression that you're not, then you're not, in their eyes. It does no good to argue, "Oh, but I *was* listening."

Dividing Your Attention

I found myself professing "Oh, but I *was* listening" when I read a comment on an evaluation form after one of my seminars. The person recounted how, at one point during a discussion, I started riffling through my material while a participant was speaking. This individual felt that when I looked away while the fellow was speaking, I gave the impression I wasn't listening. He said it looked like I didn't care what the participant was saying. Ironically, from my perspective, I was listening intently; in fact, I was searching for an article that substantiated the valuable point the participant was making. I wanted to reinforce his observation.

The truth, though, is that the evaluation comment was exactly right. I *was* listening, but from the perspective of the person who wrote the comment, I wasn't. Worse than that, I wasn't simply looking elsewhere in the room; I was looking down at my own material. As a result, I gave this individual, and possibly others, the impression that the participant's comments didn't matter, and perhaps that theirs didn't matter either.

What gives this situation broad relevance is that what I did took no more than thirty seconds, yet it made an impression that may have affected the participants' perception of me, and possibly their perception of the quality of the entire seminar. Listening, I was reminded, is more than just hearing.

Closing a Conversation

It doesn't take thirty seconds for the appearance of non-listening to cause offense, though. You can do it in less than one second. For example, a woman told me of a situation in which a conference speaker was chatting with people during the cocktail hour following a presentation he had made. The woman said that she had been talking to him when he abruptly turned away and started talking to someone else. Not that he'd cut her off in mid-sentence. She had finished what she was saying, but had intended to say something else. Whether he was aware of this or not, she didn't know, but it was clear that she was offended. She felt he couldn't be bothered with her views and had treated her accordingly.

Could it be, I asked, that he simply didn't wait those additional few nanoseconds that bring an interaction comfortably to closure, thus inadvertently giving the impression that he couldn't wait to escape? She acknowledged it was a possibility but didn't seem to care. For some people, feeling they've been snubbed packs a punch.

In closing my conversation with this woman, I stayed for several extra nanoseconds just to be safe, because her reaction had made me wonder: How often do we all do similarly innocuous things when others are speaking, and offend them in the process? And how often does the offended person not give us a chance to make it right?

Testing Your Tolerance

It's easy to make light of people's sensitivities to non-listening until you experience it yourself. Here's a simple, one-minute exercise. Pair up with someone. One of you take the role of the speaker and the other, the listener. The speaker should talk for one minute on a subject of particular interest. The listener's role is to be as visibly bored, distracted, and preoccupied as possible. After one minute, switch roles, and repeat the exercise.

People who role-play as non-listeners are very creative; for some, it's a chance to act in ways they've sometimes wished they could in work-related situations. The role of speaker, however, is much more difficult. When I've conducted this exercise with large groups, many people have commented that when they felt their partner wasn't listening, they felt discouraged from speaking. This reaction is typical, even though everyone knows it's a contrived exercise designed to make a point.

The first time I tried this exercise myself, I found my partner's "arrogance" in not listening to me unsettling. I had something to say, and I wanted his attention. Some people who try the exercise find that the other person's distracted behavior made them fight even harder for attention. Customers, however, might not be so motivated.

After you try this exercise and experience firsthand the feeling of being ignored, think about whether you inadvertently exhibit signs of non-listening when you work with customers. Giving them the impression that you are distracted or uninterested can undermine your ability to work together effectively.

DEMONSTRATING LISTENING

To improve the skill of appearing to listen, and to better appreciate the signs of both listening and not listening, observe others as they listen.

Eye Contact

For many people, eye contact with the speaker is the most persuasive indicator that someone is listening, but not everyone prefers to listen by gazing intently on the speaker. In fact, it's by looking away from the speaker that some people can best absorb what's being said. Howard occasionally listens that way. Sometimes when I'm talking to him, he has his face buried in the newspaper.

"Listen to me! I'm talking to you!" I shout.

"I *am* listening," he responds, knowing this script well and looking up from his paper only long enough to respond. This is frustrating because it doesn't look like he's listening. Still, I have no choice but to believe him, since he is usually able to precisely repeat what I said, even days later. I therefore infer that the faster he turns the pages, the more closely he's listening. It's only when he gets to the crossword puzzle and interrupts me for help in finding a word that I begin to have doubts.

Responsive Behavior

Like eye contact, body posture can convey information about listening or non-listening. People who study body language point out that leaning forward is a sign of listening and receptivity to the message. But that doesn't necessarily mean that leaning back in your chair with your arms folded suggests that you're resisting the message. For me, the configuration of the listener relative to the nearest piece of furniture is much less important than eye contact. Some of your customers, however, may feel differently.

Other indicators of listening include these:

• **Acknowledgment.** Almost as important as eye contact is acknowledgment by the listener, such as by a nod of the head, an occasional "uh-huh" or "mmmmm," or the interrogatory version, "mmmmm?" These are all forms of feedback that tell the person speaking you're paying attention. Not offering any form of acknowledgment may give the impression that you're not listening, and may make the speaker uncomfortable.

• **Questions.** Asking questions certainly indicates listening, provided the questions pertain to what has been said. "Oh, did you say something?" doesn't count. Similarly, confirming statements, in which you restate what you've heard, let the speaker know you're paying attention. Acknowledgments, questions, and confirming statements are particularly important during telephone conversations, when the visible signs of listening are unavailable.

• **Facial expression.** Professional speakers know that a blank expression on the faces of listeners doesn't necessarily mean they're not listening. It may signal just the opposite: that they're completely absorbed in listening. Nevertheless, it's the listeners who smile or in some other way visibly express interest or eagerness in what is being said that catch the speaker's attention. Even a puzzled look or a frown, unpleasant as it may be to the speaker, indicates you're listening.

• **Note-taking.** Although it requires looking away from the speaker, note-taking is a clear sign of listening. Be aware, however, that because note-taking can be distracting to the speaker, it's a courtesy to request permission to do so. The very request for permission signals your intent to listen carefully.

Moderation

Because people who feel they are being listened to are more inclined to talk, simply sitting quietly and listening can be one of the most effective ways to gather information. However, in using these techniques, don't go to extremes; overdoing it can be worse than underdoing it. When I've conducted exercises to illustrate exaggerated listening (the reverse of the non-listening exercise), participants have commented that they found it distracting to speak to overeager listeners and had a hard time concentrating on what they were saying. In using these techniques to show that you are listening, be selective as to how much responsiveness is appropriate.

LISTENING ACTIVELY

Because it's so easy for one's mind to wander, much of the listening people do is passive listening. You hear, but you may not always absorb what you're hearing. Or you hear, but you discard anything that differs from your own previously formed opinions.

Listening conscientiously and attentively is sometimes referred to as active listening, or listening for understanding. Hein van Steenis describes active listening as understanding what someone says "without being influenced by what you hear." As he points out, active listening is most difficult when you strongly disagree with the speaker's viewpoint.[1]

Techniques such as asking questions, restating what you've heard, minimizing distractions, and taking notes can be as helpful in making sure that you do listen as they are in simply demonstrating that you are listening.

Listen Before Drawing Conclusions

When you are in the habit of interrupting, your mind tends to focus on what you will say next, and not on what the speaker is saying. In his book, *Help! The Art of Computer Technical Support,* Ralph Wilson states that when he focuses fully on the matter at hand, listens carefully to a caller's words and tone of voice, and lets his mind fully engage in the caller's problem, he is able to handle even the most difficult technical problems and the most difficult people.[2]

When you jump to conclusions about either the person or what the person is saying, you are likely to then pay attention only to comments that support your conclusions and to ignore all others. This is selective listening, and it can pose problems when it's important to learn as much as you can before drawing conclusions about customers' needs. Furthermore, if you jump to conclusions, you may be less inclined to revise your conclusions later on, even if they prove to be false.

You may be prone to selective listening both with customers you especially like and those you dislike: It's easy to accept without question the ideas and the reasoning of those you like, even if flaws in their thinking become evident. It's also easy to dismiss the ideas and the reasoning of those you dislike, even when these views have merit. Jumping to conclusions makes you less able to identify and be objective about the needs of either, and reduces your ability to meet expectations.

Listen to Customers' Questions

A critical aspect of active listening is to listen carefully to your customers' questions. Doing so not only ensures you answer the questions they are really asking, but also keeps you from annoying them, as my doctor annoyed me once when I asked whether condition A ever causes condition B.

This doctor—the one who found me "unremarkable"— knew a lot about the subject, I discovered, as he proceeded to describe the findings of the last several decades of medical research. I appreciated the time he spent. Unfortunately, he failed to try to understand why I had asked the question— what my concerns were that led me to want this information— and instead gave me the benefit of his vast repertoire of knowledge. Knowledge that, for me at that moment, was irrelevant. Since his conclusion was that no relationship had been found between conditions A and B, he could have simply started by telling me so, and then elaborated if I wanted more information.

Technical personnel are sometimes guilty of regaling customers with extensive technical information, whether or not it has any bearing on their questions. One of my clients described a consultant who took this expertise-sharing to an extreme while configuring a customer's computer system. Perhaps imagining that his customer had asked, "Would you please tell me everything you know?" the consultant launched into a lengthy monologue, in the process explaining a great many things the customer didn't need to know. Not once did he ask if his customer had any questions. It was clear that the consultant was technically competent. However, not only did he not listen; the very concept seemed foreign to him.

The customer, it turns out, had numerous questions, but was reluctant to interrupt him. Yet in the consultant's own mind, he had done a commendable job. He couldn't understand why his customer didn't want to work with him again.

Listen for Statements of Expectations

In listening actively, be especially alert to statements of expectations. These statements are rarely explicit, but are recognizable once you develop the habit of listening for them. For example, if you've just implemented a new system, and your customer comments, "I thought it would be done Thursday," that's a statement of expectation.

Your customer might have actually meant any number of things by this comment. It may have been just a throwaway remark, signifying nothing. Or it may have signified appreciation: It's only Tuesday, and the customer didn't expect the system until Thursday. It may, however, have been a deliberate jab intended to point out a persistent failure to meet expectations. If customers' comments frequently suggest discrepancies between their expectations and your own, take note. These comments could be their way of expressing growing dissatisfaction, and could be a clue that you need to do more—before their dissatisfaction escalates out of control.

HELPING CUSTOMERS TO LISTEN

As important as it is for you to listen, it's also important for customers to listen, and according to some people, customers don't do a very good job of it. A project manager claimed, "I told them what to do and they didn't listen." And according to a supervisor in another company, "They never listen!" But when systems people complain that their customers don't listen to them, what they usually mean is one or more of the following: Customers bypass our standards. They ignore our advice. They don't give us what we need. In short, they don't do what we want them to do.

However, when I've worked with systems groups to try to account for what appeared to be their customers' failure to listen, we have often identified several ways in which these groups bore at least some of the responsibility. As we saw in Chapter 2, systems staffs sometimes give customers advice without explaining why the advice is important, so that customers either have no stake in following the advice or don't understand why they should follow it. Or, customers aren't taught *how* to perform a recommended task. In these situations, customers are likely to ignore the advice.

If it's been your experience that your customers don't listen, look within to see if you may be at least partly responsible, and talk to your customers to gain a better understanding of their perspective. You may find that it's not a case of their not listening, but rather their unwillingness to do the unreasonable.

SPEAKING THE WAY YOU LISTEN

Although the focus of this guideline is listening, keep in mind that eye contact, body language, and the other techniques for effective listening are equally pertinent to effective speaking. I recall a meeting I had with a colleague who dramatically recounted a recent experience, and as he did so, his eyes were focused over my head in the general direction of outer space.

It was as if he didn't know I was there, or didn't care who was listening, as long as he had an audience. As fascinating as his story was, I much preferred those intermittent moments during it when he did, briefly, look my way. If you want to be effective in getting your point across to customers, be sure they know that you know they're there.

"Active talking" may seem like a redundant phrase. After all, isn't talking inherently active? Not necessarily, if active talking means having a deliberate sensitivity to your own words and their impact on others. I recall hearing an executive who lacked that sensitivity; he opened a presentation with the statement, "I want to get through these initial slides, so we can get to the interesting stuff." It's unlikely he intended to suggest the initial slides would be boring, but he certainly succeeded in doing so. In speaking, sensitivity is important if your objective is to generate enthusiasm for your ideas.

OBSERVING CULTURAL DIFFERENCES

With all communication techniques, be aware of possible national and cultural differences. Do not automatically assume that the techniques described here will have the same effect everywhere in the world, or even everywhere in your own country. For example, in some cultures, eye contact may be a sign of distrust or disrespect; people expect you to look away while they are speaking, and failure to do so could lead to a negative reaction. In some parts of the world, long pauses in a discussion are not unusual; on the contrary, such periods of silence are quite common. Similarly, the use of body language, acknowledgment, and other techniques may differ in various parts of the world from those described here.

If you work with customers from a diversity of cultures, or have the opportunity to visit parts of the world you are unfamiliar with, learn in advance about national and cultural differences. Take the time, while there, to observe listening and speaking styles and use what you learn to communicate with customers.[3]

LEARNING TO LISTEN

The number of courses on listening is evidence of the importance of listening skills. Fortunately, listening is not a complicated subject, and most of what it takes to listen effectively are things you already know, even if you haven't thought about them before in the context of serving and supporting customers.

I obviously knew a lot about the subject of listening even when I was a twelve-year-old at summer camp. Of course, if I'd known then what I know now, I might have started charging consulting fees much, much sooner.

NOTES

[1]Hein van Steenis, *How to Plan, Develop & Use Information Systems* (New York: Dorset House Publishing, 1990), p. 292.

[2]Ralph Wilson, *Help! The Art of Computer Technical Support* (Berkeley, Calif.: Peachpit Press, 1991), p. 77.

[3]Books that can alert you to appropriate etiquette, protocol, and jargon in other cultures include *Do's and Taboos Around the World,* edited by Roger E. Axtell, compiled by the Parker Pen Company (New York: John Wiley & Sons, 1990).

Section 2
Information Gathering

The importance of information-gathering skills in managing expectations is simply stated: You can't meet customers' expectations if you don't know what they want. Yet, finding out is rarely straightforward; you can't just ask and assume they've told you what you need to know. In fact, it's safest to assume they haven't, because what they say they need may differ from what they actually need. And you must make very certain that your expectations are as reasonable and realistic as you want theirs to be.

Guidelines 5 through 8 describe how to

5. Help customers describe their needs.

6. Become an information-gathering skeptic.

7. Understand your customers' context.

8. Try the solution on for size.

5

Help Customers
Describe Their Needs

Use the "That's not it" strategy

One day, Mike, my IS director, rushed into my office and said he needed a report generated as quickly as possible from the company's database. He rapidly sketched a bunch of circles and boxes on my blackboard, drew some arrows connecting them, and announced that the logic he had diagrammed would produce the report he wanted. Before I had a chance to ask a single question, he was gone.

Because Mike was a savvy computer old-timer who could write the history of computing from firsthand experience, I was confident that not a single question would need to be asked. After all, he had been personally involved in designing the database, and he knew its idiosyncrasies well.

However, when my staff reviewed Mike's scrawled flow-chart, they concluded that his logic would not produce the output he wanted. In fact, the resulting report would have been meaningless. My staff tracked Mike down, asked a few questions, and then generated the report he really wanted, not the one he had requested.

Mike thought he had described what he wanted. Yet, he was like people everywhere who sometimes misjudge or misstate their requirements. Such foibles are universal human traits, not failings on the part of Mike or your customers—or you when you are in similar situations.

ANALYSIS WITH FOCAL POINTS

Frustration concerning customers who don't know what they want is widespread among those who serve and support customers. If you share this frustration, you have two choices: You can maintain unrealistic expectations that your next encounter with your customers will be different—or you can focus your efforts on helping customers do a better job of describing their needs. The latter choice, I firmly believe, is the wiser of the two, because it will enable both you and your customers to bring expectations more closely in line with what is reasonably and realistically feasible.

Offering customers something that resembles what they want—a focal point—is a powerful way to help customers articulate their requirements.[1] Given a focal point, they can kick it around, mold it, reshape it, and use it as a basis for saying, "That's not it, but what I *do* want is this."

Saying That's Not It

Actually, it was a travel experience that focused my thinking on the power of using this focal-point approach. I like to think of myself as a seasoned traveler who can remain calm in trying circumstances, but I didn't feel so calm the first time I went to point A and my luggage went to point B. As I waited in line at the service counter, I wondered whether I could describe my luggage precisely enough for it to be located. But before I could say a word, the service representative pulled out a laminated chart that contained a grid, four across and five down, and in each of the twenty positions was a photo of a suitcase. "Look at these photos," she said, "and tell me which suitcase looks most like yours."

I was relieved. I wouldn't need to describe my luggage. Photo #1, in the top left corner, showed a suitcase that looked vaguely like mine, but it was a different size, shape, and color. I scanned the other nineteen photos, but none of the others showed luggage similar to mine. "The first one is the closest," I told her, wondering how she was going to locate my suitcase given that it didn't really look much like the one shown in Photo #1; it was merely closer to this one than it was to any of the others.

The woman circled the appropriate number on her Missing Luggage form. Then she said, "OK, now tell me how your suitcase differs from this one." *How it differs from this one.* She didn't ask me to describe my suitcase; she asked how it differed from one that looked vaguely like it. In so doing, she gave me a focal point to use in describing my own suitcase. I told her the differences: "Mine is bigger; it's red, not blue; it has rounded corners, not sharp edges; and it has a strap around it." When she finished jotting down the differences, she had a near-perfect description of my suitcase.

When the next flight arrived from point B, the service representative recognized my suitcase the instant it came into view—and I learned a valuable technique. (Of course, I like to think that if I had gone to point B and my luggage to point A, my luggage would have gone to the service counter, looked at a chart, and explained, "She looks like the person shown in Photo #1, but she's shorter, and . . . much, much cuter.")

Missing a Focal Point

The value of using a focal point became even clearer on a sub-sequent trip, when I heard a passenger report missing luggage to an airline that didn't use this approach. The service representative asked the passenger what his luggage looked like. His response: "One bag's blue and one's brown."

The service representative looked frustrated, and asked, "Isn't there anything else you can tell me about them?"

"No," he said, "they are brown and blue suitcases."

It soon became apparent that he was visiting from a foreign country, and wasn't proficient in English. Nevertheless, the service representative didn't offer him any clues that would help him improve his description.

The contrast with my own experience was striking. Then, just as I was about to intervene, someone else did so, asking, "Are your suitcases made of a hard or soft material?" The passenger understood the question, and was able to respond, "They are soft," and then gestured to indicate their size. Photos undoubtedly would have prompted more complete descriptions, but even a single question about a single feature served as a focal point that helped to improve the description.

TECHNIQUES FOR DESCRIBING NEEDS

Focal points help customers describe things because it's easier to compare two objects than to describe an object from scratch. But besides this lesson, these luggage experiences offer several techniques for helping customers describe their needs.

1. Factor stress into your interpretation of customers' descriptions. For me, losing luggage is stressful. But whatever the provoking situation, people under stress are not necessarily able to coherently describe their needs. Despite the best of intentions, their descriptions may omit essential details or deviate considerably from the desired item or optimal solution. In the case of lost luggage, it could lead airline personnel to search in vain for luggage that matches a faulty or inadequate description.

Similarly, customers often feel stress when you ask them to describe or document their needs. This reaction may be because they needed a solution yesterday, and pressure to deliver is mounting. It may be because their priorities (like yours) change every ten minutes, and each such change affects what they are asking you to do. And it may be because dealing with specialists is often stressful, especially if their previous attempts to describe their needs failed.

2. Allow for the difficulty of describing things. A faulty description can lead to inappropriate action if the description is assumed to be accurate. Can you describe your suitcase accurately? the layout of your department? a reflection in a lake? Some people can't visualize what they're trying to describe. Others have difficulty describing things accurately, even if they can visualize them. Some people have a knack for both visualization and description but, like the traveler with the missing blue and brown luggage, lack the ability to communicate in a language familiar to those who need the description.[2]

For all these reasons, the language of description is one at which not all people excel. Therefore, it is unrealistic to expect such people to be able to describe something as conceptual and abstract as their business needs so that these needs can be flawlessly translated into solutions. A focal point can help those who lack the necessary visualization, description, or language skills.

3. Put the most likely option first. Probably eighty-five percent of all suitcases are more like the one in Photo #1 than those in the other photos, and the remaining fifteen percent are different enough to require separate photos to capture the features that make them different. So I doubt that it was coincidental that the first photo was the one most similar to my suitcase. Whenever it's feasible to present customers with a selection of choices, placing the most familiar or most desirable choice first may accelerate that process.

4. Offer categories of descriptions. People who lack a visual orientation, a facility for description, or familiarity with a particular object may not know what features best describe it.

You can help your customers by focusing their attention on relevant categories of information.[3]

5. Provide a shared language. Focal points form a context that both you and your customers can point to and discuss in terms of similarities and differences, eliminating the risk of relying strictly on your customer's use of his or her own language and your interpretation of that language.

These sagas of wayward luggage demonstrate that a picture can help you accomplish what words alone may not. These experiences also suggest that you're more likely to understand requirements if, instead of asking customers for a description, you give them a focal point as a basis for providing that description. You'll be helping them, but you'll also be helping yourself by gaining a clearer picture of what they want you to accomplish for them.

TYPES OF FOCAL POINTS

The focal point you use depends on what you're trying to accomplish, but almost anything that offers a concrete starting point can be helpful. It could be a set of sample report layouts, a proposed network configuration, a library of sample correspondence, a portfolio of sample graphs, a brief segment of a videotaped course, or a selection of menu formats.

For example, a technical specialist whose job is to help customers justify their hardware and software purchases might offer a set of descriptions of departmental applications already in use in the company. The focal point can be any element of a system or solution that helps customers begin to appreciate the possibilities and articulate what they need.

Prototypes as Focal Points

Providing a focal point is what the concept of prototyping is all about. It enables you to start with something that lets you and your customers see, through successive approximations, how a solution will look and function before you invest time and effort to produce or obtain it. Prototyping provides a way to reach a consensus on requirements. In Chapter 8, we'll see how prototypes can facilitate consensus on a solution.

But prototyping often starts with a blank sheet of paper or a blank computer screen. The prototyping process can benefit from using focal points to reveal needs that might otherwise remain hidden until it's too late. Focal points may help you accelerate the process and focus more accurately on relevant features.

Report layouts are a good example. Given a sample report, customers can identify those aspects of it that most closely reflect what they'd like, and they can itemize the ways in which they'd like their own to differ. And given a selection of reports with varying features, customers can tell you even more about what they want. You can go a step further by itemizing some of the features they may want to consider: orientation, layout, spacing, graphical options, and so on. By developing a prototype report that combines the features identified as pertinent, you and your customers then have a concrete basis for further assessment. For customers who do their own report generation, a kit of sample report formats would familiarize them with options they might not think of otherwise.

Service Requests as Focal Points

Even a service request prepared by a customer can serve as a focal point. The process of documenting and reviewing the request can lead to a closer approximation of what the customer wants. Frederick Brooks supports formal documents for just that reason. As he notes, the act of writing requires hundreds of small decisions, which help to reveal gaps and inconsistencies in one's thinking.[4]

Therefore, by viewing customers' service requests as a focal point, you can use these requests themselves as a basis for working with customers to help identify similarities or differences that will more precisely target what is actually needed. If you modify your own expectations, so that you not only expect customers to revise their initial request but actively *encourage* them to do so, you will acquire a clearer picture of their needs, and you'll have it earlier in the effort than if you resist or resent such revisions.

Bargaining Chips as Focal Points

Now, think about extending this focal-point concept to planning or negotiating efforts. For example, suppose you are negotiating a contract with a vendor or developing a service agreement with customers. Instead of presenting the other party with a blank sheet and asking what services or features they'd like, propose those that best describe your own needs or ability to deliver. This creates a point from which they can say, "That's not feasible, but . . ." An added benefit is that the reaction of the other party is often one of accepting the starting point you've specified. Therefore, by providing a focal point, you actually simplify the negotiation process.

PITFALLS OF FOCAL POINTS

No strategy is perfect, and in certain situations, focal points can backfire. It did with one of my customers, Charlie, the division manager discussed in Chapter 3. Charlie's experiences with IS had been, in his view, highly unsatisfactory. Long before the incident with Nathan and the dinner meeting, it was clear he expected to be disappointed with the system we were developing. We were determined to prove him wrong; in the meantime, our relationship was dominated by tension.

Based on the specifications his staff had given us for the system, we prepared two proposals. Each would provide a strong foundation for meeting the division's needs, but the two differed significantly in the impact they would have on the division's work flow and the distribution of responsibilities. We could have offered just one approach, but we had decided to try to defuse the tension between us and build trust. Our plan was to invite Charlie and his staff to select their preferred alternative, and to tell us how that choice could be modified to better meet their needs.

We met in a conference room near my office. Charlie arrived with an entourage of division staff. As the meeting got under way, I remember thinking that it would have been politically wiser to have met on his turf. My project manager began her presentation of the two alternatives and the pluses and minuses of each. But we were not to hear the end of it—literally—because midway through, Charlie stood up and shouted, "How dare you consider alternatives without our input?"

Our objective had been to do exactly that: to encourage their input and to have them tell us how they wanted it done. Our proposals, we felt, would provide a focal point for discussion and a means for us to show how receptive we were to their views. Charlie was so incensed about his division not being involved in formulating these proposals that he rejected both of them, proving that giving customers something to start with doesn't always work.

Possibly Charlie felt we were offering a choice of two done deals, neither of which could possibly meet his staff's needs because they didn't have any say about either alternative. Although we eventually negotiated a project plan, Charlie's initial misinterpretation of the focal points was an unfortunate obstacle.

THINKING WITH FOCAL POINTS

If your customers' vague descriptions of what they want makes it tough to meet their expectations, consider how you can modify your approach to help them do a better job:

- Think about situations in which you might have done a better job of identifying needs if you had given customers a focal point to discuss.

- Brainstorm with your coworkers about things you might use as focal points—and invite your customers to suggest some of their own ideas. Consider ways in which you can use multiple focal points, such as a set of pictures or descriptions, so that customers can comment on what they like or don't like about each.

- Describe to your customers the benefits of expressing their needs in terms of similarities and differences.

- Keep in mind that identifying what customers don't want is as important as identifying what they do want.

- Ask customers questions that will expand their view of relevant features.

Finding More Focal Points

Once focal-point thinking becomes routine, let your everyday experiences guide you in refining the process. For example, when I visited my brother, he asked what my suitcase looked like so he could retrieve it from the baggage carousel. Well-versed at this by now, I quickly recited: "Medium size, light brown, hard-sided, with a blue strap around it." As one that perfectly matched my description came into view, he exclaimed, "There it is!"

The only problem was that the suitcase wasn't mine! True, it was medium size, light brown, and hard-sided, just like mine, but the blue strap? Yes, it had one, but the strap was fastened around the length of the suitcase,

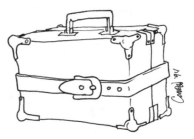

instead of the width.

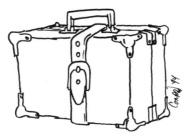

I, of course, knew immediately that it wasn't mine. That's when I learned another important lesson: Descriptions can be detailed and accurate, but still ambiguous. Don't let a description that sounds perfect keep you from ensuring that your understanding matches your customers'.

Give your customers a chance to tell you what I told my brother: That's not it, but . . .

NOTES

[1]As Gause and Weinberg point out, "In spite of appearances, people seldom know what they want until you give them what they ask for." Donald C. Gause and Gerald M. Weinberg, *Are Your Lights On?* (New York: Dorset House Publishing, 1990), p. 143.

[2]Donald Norman notes that people don't normally need precise memory information. He states, "It is a general property of memory that we store only partial descriptions of the things to be remembered, descriptions that are sufficiently precise to work at the time something is learned, but that may not work later on, when new experiences have also been encountered and entered into the memory." Donald A. Norman, *The Design of Everyday Things* (New York: Basic Books, 1988), p. 59.

[3]Donald Norman describes how he differentiates between notebooks: If he keeps his notes in a small red notebook, and it's his only notebook, he describes it simply as his notebook. But if he buys several more note-books, then the earlier description is no longer adequate, and he must call the first one small or red, or perhaps both, to distinguish it from the new ones. And if he acquires several small, red notebooks, it becomes necessary to use other means of describing the first notebook, so as to be able to distinguish it from the others. See Norman, loc. cit.

[4]Frederick P. Brooks, Jr., *The Mythical Man-Month* (Reading, Mass.: Addison-Wesley Publishing Co., 1975), p. 111.

6

Become an Information-Gathering Skeptic

Challenge your assumptions

Suppose a customer submits a request to you for an XYZ. "Terrific," you say, "I'll produce one for you." You produce a spectacular XYZ, implement it, and parade it before your customer, proud of the splendid job you did. Your customer takes one look at it and says, "That's not what I wanted." You're puzzled, because you know you did what he asked. Did you meet your customer's expectations? Apparently not.

As discussed in the previous chapter, focal points can help you develop an understanding of customers' needs. Although focal points provide an excellent place to start, you need to do some information gathering to refine your understanding. That means becoming not just an information-gathering specialist, but also an information-gathering skeptic. It is your role to be a skeptic, not because customers deliberately try to mislead you, but because they might not say what they mean. If you don't do a good job of determining what they really need, your attempts to meet their expectations may fail. This guideline provides ideas and pointers that will help you excel as an information-gathering skeptic.[1]

LEARN FROM A MODEL SKEPTIC

An important step in becoming an information-gathering skeptic is to develop a questioning frame of mind. Ask lots of questions, but don't limit your questions to things you don't know. Ask questions even if you feel you already know all about the customer you're gathering information from and the problems you've been asked to address. Don't act like you know it all, even if you're convinced you do. In fact, try just the reverse. That's what Columbo would do.

Columbo is the rumpled TV detective who always has just one more question. Even when he has most of the answers, he asks another question, and then another. Each question draws out a bit more information. Interestingly, suspects (or customers, in your case) often reveal much more information in responding than they realize. And often, they answer questions that weren't specifically asked but that can be instrumental in solving the problem. Donning a trench coat, driving a beat-up car, and acting befuddled may be more than is called for, but you'll learn more if you don't come across as the expert. If you prompt customers to provide information, you'll end up with far more than you anticipated.

CLARIFY SERVICE REQUESTS

Let's look at the case of someone who didn't know about the Columbo approach: A trainer named Tanya visited a remote site, at her customer's request, to talk about some training the department wanted. When Tanya asked the department manager what was needed, the answer was "advanced spreadsheet training." Tanya went back to her office to develop the requested course.

When she returned several weeks later and presented the course she had so painstakingly developed, she was met by puzzled stares. It would be an exaggeration to say her customers didn't understand a single word, because they understood just fine when she said, "Let's take a break." But the course material she provided clearly confused them.

Why, Tanya wondered, had they asked for advanced training, when they clearly weren't ready for it? Unfortunately, Tanya had misjudged the department's needs. As a result, the class was a waste of time and led the department manager to feel that, although she and Tanya had agreed on what was needed, Tanya had provided something else. No wonder this experience seriously lowered the manager's confidence in the training department's ability to understand its customers.

The class was a complete waste of Tanya's time, too, and reinforced her conviction that customers are incapable of describing their needs. Yet she hadn't asked any questions that would have helped her clarify her understanding of those needs.

CHALLENGE YOUR ASSUMPTIONS

Tanya might have benefited by asking herself, Do they have expectations about the form the training will take, based on past experiences with training? What leads me to think they will understand the instruction I provide? Tanya might also have asked herself, Are there certain tasks they expect to be able to do after this training?

Tanya assumed her customers knew how to assess their technical proficiency. Yet, assessing technical proficiency was her job, not theirs. She also assumed her customers knew how to translate their proficiency level into a request for training. Yet, they weren't trainers, and didn't know about course offerings and training options. Perhaps worst of all, Tanya assumed that what her customers meant by advanced training matched what she meant by it.

What should Tanya have done—and what can you do—to test such assumptions and develop a better understanding of customers' needs? Consider the following suggestions:

• **Take nothing at face value.** No matter what your customers tell you, don't assume they said what they meant, or meant what they said. Ask questions and more questions.[2] Even repeat questions you've already asked, rephrasing them from a different perspective.

For example, after asking about what tasks the customers would be able to undertake as a result of the training, Tanya could have asked about the benefits the requested training would provide, and about the business needs the training would help address. All three questions focus on training outcomes, but from a slightly different perspective, and each of these questions might have further expanded her understanding of what she had already learned during the interview.

Asking additional questions might have also helped Tanya to identify other related problems that her customers hadn't thought to mention initially. If she had asked her customers to describe the most difficult spreadsheet problem they'd encountered, or the spreadsheet features they found most valuable, she might have learned not only about their technical proficiency with spreadsheets, but their upcoming needs for other types of training. All these questions would have yielded additional information that could have steered her in the right direction.

• **Ask for clarification.** If you're a serious information-gathering skeptic, you miss no opportunity to ask customers to clarify what they mean. When a customer requests "advanced spreadsheet training," for example, a bell should go off in your head that causes you to ask, "What do you mean by advanced? Do you mean mammoth macros? complex calculations? grandiose graphs? Or do you mean simple sums?" Harvey Brightman stresses the importance of being skeptical of the language used to describe a problem situation. Question all "facts," he urges us, and don't confuse opinion with fact.[3]

• **Don't be concerned about appearing unprepared.** You may fear that customers will view you as unprepared or incapable of doing your job if you ask for clarification. However, you will not lose face by explicitly telling customers that you want to be sure you understand what they need. In fact, the needs assessment process is an ideal one in which to raise the issue of expectations, and to explain to your customers how important your questions are to ensure you fully understand their expectations.

• **Ask concrete questions.** Ralph Wilson recommends asking very concrete questions when seeking clarification about a technical problem.[4] The value of this recommendation was revealed in one of my workshops in which we were discussing Tanya-like assumptions that participants had made. One technical support specialist described a customer who called to report that her PC screen was blank. This being one of the most familiar of all problems that technical support groups experience, the specialist took the customer's description of the problem at face value and began to list the likely explanations. Only after lengthy questioning did the specialist realize that the caller's screen was not blank at all. It was filled with systems-level information and was merely missing some customer data the caller thought should be displayed.

Among the questions that workshop participants suggested to more quickly diagnose this situation were "What color is your blank screen?" and "Is any pattern displayed?" These are perfect examples of concrete questions.

• **Gather information from multiple sources.** Tanya would have benefited by asking the same questions of different individuals in separate interviews, and then comparing their responses. Even within a given department, everyone views problems from a somewhat different angle, and each additional perspective can add to the overall picture. Furthermore, it can be enlightening to present similar questions to managers and staff in separate interviews, because there are often differences between these groups' responses. Such differences can provide a broader perspective of needs than questioning only managers or only staff, or by interviewing all of them together, as Tanya did.

Feedback from multiple sources helps to fill in the gaps in what any given source tells you. For example, in preparing a presentation to company management on computing opportunities and responsibilities, one of my clients interviewed the members of several departments, and asked them what they felt their managers needed to know. One financial analyst pleaded: "Please tell my manager that developing a complex application isn't an instantaneous process." This analyst was one of several who felt their managers had unrealistic expectations.

• **Consider the source.** Whether you gather information from one source or many, you must take into account the capabilities and perspectives of the individuals providing that information before you can interpret it. For example, Tanya should have tried to determine her customers' skill level. With just a few technical questions, she could easily have ascertained their readiness for advanced training. If she had scanned some applications and found evidence of circuitous or clumsy techniques, she would have quickly realized their skill level, and interpreted their responses accordingly. Instead, she simply accepted their request as stated.

ALLOW FOR INACCURACY

Customers generally respond to information-gathering questions correctly and accurately, based on their own perspective. The department manager didn't intentionally mislead Tanya. Yet, in the case of failure, shouldn't customers be held responsible for responses that are incorrect or inaccurate?

Consider, for example, a familiar experience in technical support: The customer has a technical problem and calls you for help. The customer describes the problem in customer terms, "My blankety-blank isn't working." You ask, "Did you try the whatchamacallit?" The customer responds, "Yes, but it didn't help." You ask additional questions, but get nowhere, so you go to the customer area and try the blankety-blank yourself. You discover that some of your customer's answers were incorrect. Correct answers would have led you to the source of the problem, but the customer's description misled you. In your own mind, you call the customer a liar. But was he really?

I found out how it feels to be in the customer's shoes shortly after Howard and I bought a new car. When it wouldn't start, I thought, Hmmm, it's not just a new car, it's a new dead car. After many tries, I finally succeeded in starting the car. This happened to me several times that week. I told Howard something was wrong with the car, but he disagreed because he never had a problem with it.

One day, we both got in the car. I tried to start it, and it wouldn't start. I gave Howard my I-told-you-so look. He asked if I had pressed down on the clutch pedal while I turned the key. I had. "Are you sure?" he asked. I was sure. "Are you *positive?*" he asked.

"I'm positive," I told him, with that certain smugness you get when you know you're right. I tried several more times. Nothing. We were both stumped.

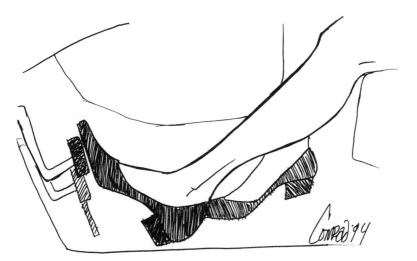

Then I tried once more, and the car started. We looked at each other in surprise and confusion. I'm a magician, I thought. I turned the car off and started it again. Then I realized what had happened. Although I had pressed down on the clutch pedal each of the previous times, I had pressed it down only to within an inch of the floor. In that position, the car wouldn't start. There was no margin for error. With the clutch pedal pressed all the way to the floor, the car started. Otherwise, it didn't.

Do customers lie when they respond with what they believe to be the truth? For most customers, not telling the truth in response to your information-gathering questions is not the same as lying. It's your job as an information-gathering skeptic to ferret out the truth, checking and double-checking that the questions they answer are the ones you asked.

POSE STRATEGIC QUESTIONS

Here are some techniques that can help you draw accurate responses from your customers.

• **Ask questions that focus on the process.** In an information-gathering situation, it's easy to inadvertently put people on the defensive, especially if you ask questions that seem to be about them, rather than their activities or problems. Therefore, focus your inquiry not on the person you're questioning, but on the process or project about which you're seeking information. For example, instead of asking, "Why did you do it this way?" ask, "What was the reason for this approach?" Or, instead of asking, "Do you ever encounter problems with this method?" ask, "What kinds of problem have occurred in using this method?" In both examples, the first question is phrased in such a way that you might appear to be challenging your customer's ability or intelligence, and you might touch on sensitivities that you know nothing about. The second question, by contrast, asks about the activity or project, and is less likely to generate defensiveness.

• **Ask questions that focus on the person.** Does this technique contradict the previous technique? No, it's simply that both process-oriented and customer-oriented questions have their place. When you ask questions such as "Do these delays complicate your job?" or "What is the most troubling aspect of this problem for you?" you are demonstrating concern for the customer. An information-gathering session typically includes a mix of both process-oriented and person-oriented questions to provide a balance between focus on the person and focus on the subject of the interview. In Chapter 7, we will discuss customer-focused questions in greater detail.

• **Ask consensus-building questions.** Consensus-building questions are process-focused; that is, they concern the information-gathering process itself and ensure it is proceeding in a manner satisfactory to the customer. Consider, for example, such questions as, "Are you with me on this?" or "Does this make sense to you?" or "Do you have any concerns about what we've discussed so far?" By asking such questions periodically during an information-gathering session, you give customers a chance to have a say about the process. Such questions reveal concerns that would otherwise escalate into major problems.[5]

• **Ask about the benefits of solutions the customer suggests.** A simple yet effective question is, "How would that help you?" This question shifts attention from *what* customers want to *why* they want it, and how they would benefit if certain actions were taken. Your tone of voice in asking this question is important. Asked improperly ("How would *that* help you?"), it could sound like a challenge, rather than a request for additional information. To reduce the risk of inadvertently sounding this way, phrase this question as a process-oriented question: "How would that be helpful?"

• **Ask "why" questions carefully.** Questions that ask why something is done a certain way might inadvertently trigger defensiveness, regardless of whether they are phrased as process-oriented or person-oriented questions. It is not necessary to suppress all "why" questions; just be aware of both the potential impact of such questions and ways you can reword them to reduce the potential of creating offense.

Consider, for example, the question, "Why is this process performed monthly instead of weekly?" The question can be softened by asking, "What is the reason for performing this process monthly instead of weekly?" You can soften it even further by asking, "Can you help me understand why this process is performed monthly instead of weekly?" Both of these questions still ask why, but they do so in a way that sounds less like an accusation and more like a need for help in understanding. Or you can simply ask, "What is the basis for this particular scheduling?"

Even when direct "why" questions seem appropriate, be careful how you ask them. Looking puzzled when you ask, "Why do you do it this way?" might cause your customer to hear it as, "How could you be so ridiculous?"

• **Ask for more than yes or no.** Questions that can be answered by a flat yes or no can divert you from understanding the problem. For example, customer service staff often ask customers who report a software problem, "Have any changes been made recently to the software?" If the caller's response is no, the tendency is to accept that response, and move on to explore other possibilities. Instead, it's better to ask open-ended questions, such as "What kinds of changes have been made to the software recently?" Questions such as this prevent yes/no responses and elicit information that may be useful in diagnosing the problem, such as by revealing changes made to the system that callers didn't view as relevant.

• **Offer observations.** The very process of asking a question sometimes "leads the witness" and influences the response. By making statements that express general observations, you can generate information beyond what you get from questions alone. For example, Tanya might have learned more if she had simply said, "This appears to be a very busy time for this department" or "It's probably difficult for you to fit in as much training as you'd like." People rarely let such statements pass without commenting, and since they will interpret these statements from their own perspective, their responses may be valuable.

• **Play back statements to ensure you understood.** By restating what you heard, you give your customer a chance to confirm your understanding, to correct it, or to add to it. For example, ask "Do I understand you to be saying that . . . ?" or "If I understand correctly, what you mean is . . ." or "I'm not sure I follow what you mean to say." Because such statements are so effective in encouraging additional information, it's useful to periodically play back statements, even if you're sure you understood what you heard. Don't overdo it, though. Prefacing every statement with "If I understand correctly . . ." is a misuse of this technique, and is more likely to stifle discussion than to promote it.

• **Invite customers to think of questions you haven't asked.** You can't possibly know all the questions you should ask, so involve customers in identifying what you've missed. By prompting them to think of additional questions, you may cause them to reveal information they hadn't thought of until that moment. Therefore, at least once near the end of a short information-gathering session, and periodically during a long session, ask, "Is there anything else you think I ought to know?" Or ask, "What other questions should I ask you now, so that we'll avoid problems later on?" Don't be surprised if they raise critical issues, past experiences, and other important details that they never thought to offer—and you never thought to ask about.

LEARN TO THINK LIKE A SKEPTIC

If you want to succeed as an information-gathering skeptic, you have to think like one. When customers give you some information, ask yourself, If I were unsure of what they're saying, what would I ask next? When you are the customer in the interaction, do exactly the same. Be like Columbo, and ask questions even when you are sure. And develop the habit of asking, "What do you mean when you say . . . ?" You may feel a little self-conscious at first, but with practice, it'll become second nature. Anyway, it's part of good detective work, and it's what a certified skeptic would do.

NOTES

[1]For additional information on how to conduct an information-gathering session, see Naomi Karten, *Mind Your Business: Strategies for Managing End-User Computing* (Wellesley, Mass.: QED Information Sciences, 1990), pp. 135-60.

[2]Harvey Brightman points out, "Frequently we hesitate to ask questions; perhaps we do not want to appear ignorant. Given a choice of being ignorant or appearing to be ignorant, many individuals will select the former. Such individuals may never suffer loss of face, but they pay a price, for the difference between success and failure in problem solving often is the amount and quality of the questions generated." Harvey J. Brightman, *Problem Solving: A Logical and Creative Approach* (Atlanta: Georgia State University, 1980), p. 48.

[3]Ibid. pp. 100-101.

[4]Ralph Wilson, *Help! The Art of Computer Technical Support* (Berkeley, Calif.: Peachpit Press, 1991), p. 124.

[5]Gause and Weinberg describe a related category of questions called metaquestions, which are questions about the questioning process. They suggest, for example, that you might ask, "Do my questions seem relevant?" or "Is there anyone else who can give me useful answers?" See Donald C. Gause and Gerald M. Weinberg, *Exploring Requirements* (New York: Dorset House Publishing, 1989), pp. 62, 63.

7

Understand Your Customers' Context

Study the problem before you solve it

If you singlemindedly focus on your customers' immediate problems, without considering them in a broader business context, you may overlook the way the problematic situation interacts with other processes and activities both in and outside the organization. Even if you succeed in solving the immediate problem, you might create another one to take its place—and the subsequent problem might be bigger than the first. Customers might reasonably view such an outcome as a failure to meet their expectations.

To prevent this type of outcome, you must ensure that information-gathering efforts examine the problem from all possible perspectives. As Donald Gause and Gerald Weinberg state, "If you can't think of at least three things that might be wrong with your understanding of the problem, you don't understand the problem."[1] For many people, this is not the customary approach.

CATEGORIZE THE CONTEXT

A variety of questions can help you think about what might be lacking in your understanding of the problem. The questions in the preceding chapter were designed to help you ask appropriate information-gathering questions. The questions in this chapter help you take into account all relevant aspects of the problem. To identify appropriate questions, start by devising categories of issues about which you might want additional information. One way to identify such categories is to use an attention-directing tool that Edward de Bono calls Consider All Factors.[2]

Consider All Factors

According to de Bono, "doing a CAF" means preparing a list of all the factors that have to be considered in a situation, without making any attempt to evaluate the factors. The resulting list of items is likely to overlap, and not to be in a priority sequence. Doing a CAF is an effective method of identifying a broader range of relevant issues than might be identified otherwise.

For example, you might determine, via a CAF or using any other means of devising categories, that four pertinent categories of questions are business, impact, timing, and risk factors. You would then formulate a series of specific questions within each of these categories to help broaden your view of the problem you have been asked to address. Sample questions for each of these four categories follow.

Business factors. These questions broaden your understanding of the business environment in which the problem has arisen.

- What financial factors contribute to this problem?

- What business factors could cause the problem to grow or change in ways so that it could be seen in a different light?

- What steps have competitors taken to address this problem?

- What business benefits might there be for leaving things as they are?

Impact factors. These questions help in understanding the factors both in and outside the requesting department that either affect or are affected by the problem.

- What areas of the company are affected by the problem?

- What business processes outside this area are affected by this situation?

- What will be the long-term impact of modifying the current process?

- Who might resist our attempts to tackle this problem?

Timing factors. These questions concern the changes in the problem over time, and the decision to address the problem now.

- When did this problem first arise, and why?

- Why has this problem not been addressed before?

- What makes this a particularly good or bad time to address this problem?

- What would be the positive and negative consequences of waiting a month or a year to address this problem?

Risk factors. These questions focus attention on negative situations that could arise in addressing the problem.

- What does the problem entail that is so new or different as to pose a risk?

- What factors might reduce the level of risk that the problem poses?

- What does past experience tell us about complications that might arise if we address this problem?

- In what ways is the risk of addressing the problem less than the risk of leaving things as they are?

Develop Your Own Questions

If you find these categories and sample questions helpful, you can formulate additional questions to guide your information-gathering efforts. Other categories of questions, such as those pertaining to training, data access, scheduling, and security, can serve equally well if they facilitate your analysis of the problem from various perspectives.

Many of these questions are ones you undoubtedly already think about, so organizing them into categories simply helps to make your thinking about them more systematic. Do not be concerned if some overlap exists between questions in different categories, or if certain questions seem to fit in more than one category. The idea, as de Bono noted, is not to generate a list of mutually exclusive categories, but to develop questions that help you stretch your thinking and expand your understanding.

Some of these questions may require you or your customers to do some hard thinking or even some research to come up with the answers, but the effort is worthwhile if it identifies even a single piece of information that changes your understanding of the problem. Such questions can be useful not just for you to ask your customers, but for customers to ask themselves before seeking your assistance. Consider compiling and distributing a list of such questions to help your customers structure their thinking about problems.

For customers who prefer to solve their own problems rather than solicit your assistance, such questions help to improve the odds that they take all relevant factors into account in developing a solution. Too often, customers overlook important factors, run into problems when the solution they devised ceases to do what they need, and then turn to you for help. By educating customers to improve their own information-gathering skills, both you and they benefit.

Draw Conclusions from the Responses

After answering these types of questions yourself or with your customers, you can ask a few additional questions to evaluate the information you've gathered and make some decisions about your next step. For example,

- What issues did these questions raise that are critical to consider in addressing the problem?

- Did these questions raise any issues that we had initially overlooked?

- Has our view of the problem changed as a result of asking these contextual questions?

- Do the responses suggest that we shouldn't address the problem in the way we had planned? If so, what should we do next?

- Do the responses suggest that we shouldn't address this problem at all?[3]

CASE STUDY: PEAK WORKLOAD

Questions that expand understanding of a problem's context could have been used to avoid the situation described in the following case: A utility company issued more than a hundred thousand bills each month. Most of the bills had first-of-the-month due dates, and were computer-generated in a single lengthy run about twenty-five days before each due date. The rest of the bills had due dates at five other points throughout the month—the fifth, tenth, fifteenth, twentieth, or twenty-fifth—and were produced in five comparatively short runs, also about twenty-five days before each due date. Because most customers sent in their payment close to the due date, the

billing process placed a considerable workload on both computer and human resources in getting the first-of-the-month
bills out and in processing first-of-the-month payments. The
billing staff wanted to even out the workload so that it was
spread throughout the month, and they wanted to accomplish
the spread by reallocating accounts evenly across the six billing
cycles.

The request came from a department that had credibility and
clout in the organization, so it was easy to unquestioningly
accept the request as stated. Besides, the problem seemed clear:
how to distribute the workload more evenly.

If this request were submitted to you, what types of contextual questions would you want to ask? You could ask any of
the previously listed business, impact, timing, or risk questions, but you might also ask questions that address a variety
of additional factors such as personnel, financial, or scheduling
issues.

When I've presented this case study as a seminar exercise, participants have listed such factors as staffing, workload distribution, problem history, financial impact, and
implementation as areas of particular interest, and have suggested such additional questions as the following:

- What was the original reason for establishing the billing process this way? Is that reason still valid?

- What other departments would be affected by a change in billing cycles?

- What kinds of savings does the current approach provide, such as postage discounts for the high-volume mailing of first-of-the-month bills?

- What are the desirable aspects of the problem?

- What need is there for temporary personnel or overtime to handle the current peak work-load?

- How long has this situation been a problem? Why has it not been addressed before?

- How would a distribution of payments throughout the month affect the company's cash flow?

- How does computer processing currently accommodate the lengthy billing run each month without negative impact on other processing?

- How would the company's customers be affected by a shift to a different billing cycle? How should they be advised and prepared?

- Who outside the billing department views this situation as a problem?

- Who might find the current approach preferable?

These questions are typical in that they constitute a mix of two types of questions: First are those that focus on the specific problem; second are questions that pertain more generally to any problem, such as those that ask who views the situation as a problem, who might prefer to keep things as they are, and what the desirable aspects of the problem are. All of these questions help define the problem. As Gause and Weinberg note, "Without some common understanding of the problem, a solution will almost invariably be to the wrong problem."[4]

Group Brainstorming

Whenever I've used this type of case-study exercise in my seminars, I've found that people working in groups develop more pertinent questions than they do working individually.

It is clear that group brainstorming provides an effective catalyst for expectations management. It's also clear that all members of the group need not have firsthand knowledge either of the specific business environment or of the system problem in order to identify appropriate questions. In fact, participants in companies most like the case-study company usually generate the narrowest range of questions, perhaps because they're too familiar with the context. The objectivity of those least familiar with a problem sometimes leads to the best examination. Therefore, as suggested in Chapter 6, if you want to learn as much as possible about a customer's problem, draw upon as many resources as you can, seeking the input of both those familiar and unfamiliar with the problem.

To further benefit from this technique, involve your customers in developing these questions, and encourage them to formulate some of their own. By making this question-generating process a joint effort as well as a routine part of your problem-solving methodology, you will improve the odds of a successful outcome. And in some cases, that outcome may include the determination that your customers' original expectations were not realistic, and needed to be modified. At least, that was the case with the billing system request.

Unforeseen Interconnections

Any of these previously listed questions would have been valuable to ask at the start of the billing project on which this case study is based, but none were asked. Not only was the problem not explored in greater depth, but the reaction of numerous people who heard that modifications were being undertaken was, "It's about time!" Everyone viewed the problem as straightforward. No one assumed the role of information-gathering skeptic. No one suggested that it might be wise to first evaluate the possible consequences of tackling the problem. Everyone, later on, wished they had.

In fact, the modifications turned out to have wide-ranging negative impact—on numerous computer systems, on operating procedures both in and outside the billing department, and on the utility company's public image. By the time these major, previously unforeseen complications became apparent, it was several months into the system modification effort, and also well into the efforts of several departments to prepare for the new system.

As the project proceeded, it became increasingly clear that the "problem" only existed when viewed within the narrow context of the billing department's staffing needs. But this problem, real though it was, was trivial by contrast with the negative consequences that would likely emerge if the company implemented the planned solution. Finally, after several slips in the implementation date while trying to tie off yet another loose end, systems staff and customers jointly agreed to terminate the project.

FOCUS ON THE CUSTOMER

In addition to improving your understanding of the problem, information gathering can be used to learn more about your customers' expectations and how they view their responsibilities. Questions that focus on the customer, rather than the problem or immediate objective, can sometimes generate more information than any other method. Why? Because, people rarely have an opportunity to talk about themselves, and when given that opportunity, many take full advantage of it. In the process, they often provide more information about problems you are being (or will be) asked to address than if you questioned them specifically about those problems.

Questioning Strategies

To illustrate the value of customer-focused questions to the participants of a consulting skills seminar, I decided to run a two-part experiment in which they unknowingly participated. In interviewing them several weeks before the seminar to assess their needs and customize my material, I first asked each participant questions regarding my immediate objective: the class. I asked, for example, "What do you want to get out of the class?" and "What topics do you want this class to focus on?" Their responses varied from brief statements to "Gee, I don't know." None of the participants' answers provided detailed information about their needs.

But that was just the first part of my experiment. For part two, I told them to forget the questions I had just asked, because I had others I wanted to ask them. Then, instead of asking questions regarding my immediate objective, I focused my questions on them: their problems, their concerns, their environment. I asked each of them questions such as: What is a typical day like for you? What problems do you experience in identifying customer needs? Have your customers ever given you information that later proved to be incomplete? Do they ever misunderstand your instructions?

If I hadn't cut off their responses, they'd still be talking today. Given the opportunity to focus on familiar problems and everyday experiences, they overflowed with information. In the process of responding to my questions, they talked about problems in establishing priorities amidst conflicting demands. They described conflicts they had with other groups, which hampered their ability to meet their commitments. They explained the difficulties they faced due to staffing constraints. To a degree that would impress even Columbo, they told me about their organization, their division, and their day-to-day challenges. What they told me was exactly what I needed in order to understand their environment and to tailor the seminar to their needs.

Of the several class participants, one in particular stood out. This woman talked nonstop for half an hour after I asked her only one question: What are some of the problems you experience in working with customers? In responding, she not only answered all my questions in considerable detail; she also answered a few I hadn't thought to ask.

As it turned out, she really was a talkaholic, who took great pride in her ability to talk endlessly (her colleagues concurred when I revealed the details of my experiment during the seminar). Nevertheless, when I initially asked her what she wanted to get out of the seminar, she said she had no idea. The contrast between her responses validated my views about the value of customer-focused questions in information gathering.

Talk-Inducing Topics

The more you learn about the context in which your customers work—and how they perceive that context—the better you'll understand their problems and identify appropriate solutions. Learning about your customers' context turns out to be relatively easy: Simply ask about their frustrations, concerns, and priorities. Ask what's working and what's not. Ask what's making them happy and what's driving them crazy.

These questions may sound irrelevant, yet they are extremely effective in stimulating the flow of ideas and can help you serve your customers long after the immediate problem has been resolved. And you don't have to wait until you're addressing a specific problem to ask these questions. In fact, the best time to use these questions is in information-gathering meetings designed not to address specific problems, but to discuss changing needs and priorities. Furthermore, these questions generate considerable feedback from both new and long-time customers.

If you're concerned that your customers may be reluctant to open up, simply start by asking them to describe a typical day or some of the problems they experience in doing their job. Both questions are proven talk-inducing approaches. In my experience, the problem isn't getting people to start talking, but getting them to stop. In fact, it's a good idea to have a mutually determined ending time before the meeting begins.

The following paragraphs summarize ways to expand your understanding of your customers. Be sure to ask your most important questions first, in case you run out of time before you get to the rest. As my talkaholic student demonstrated, a good first question can eliminate the need for any other.

• **What causes your priorities to change?** Have your customers identify two or three key factors that make priorities change. Ask how these changes in priorities take place. Of the factors your customers describe, ask which they have some control over and which they see as beyond their control. As you listen to their responses, be sensitive to issues they describe that might make it hard for you to succeed in meeting their expectations, no matter what solution you devise.

• **What's unique about this department?** Find out what they view as unique about their own responsibilities and their staff's. Ask what aspects of their work they find particularly frustrating, and what (or who) gets in their way and makes it hard for them to meet their obligations. People often believe that their work is more tedious, demanding, and pressured than everyone else's. Whether you agree with their view is unimportant. What you're seeking is their perspective, because it could have direct bearing on the solution you recommend.

• **What interactions do you have with other departments or with outside organizations?** Understanding the flow of information (both electronic and human) into and out of a business unit can be useful not just for your immediate effort, but also to gain a general understanding of the relationship between these customers and the others with whom they have contact. Search the implications of this information for ways to help resolve their problems.

• **What would you like to change in this department?** Of course, some things aren't changeable, but answers to this question can give you some useful insight into the functioning of the area. Talk to several people in a department about what they'd like to change, what they consider inefficient, and what they find tedious. The similarities or differences in their responses will tell you a great deal about trouble spots, sources of resistance, and factors you might want to keep in mind in responding to their needs.

• **What would you like to keep the same in this department?** If your job is to implement change, it is easy to see everything as needing change. To avoid this viewpoint, it is helpful to inquire specifically about what people in the department would like to preserve. As with the previous question, the similarities and differences in the responses of several members of the department may reveal both opportunities and risks in addressing their needs.

• **What kinds of situations make it difficult to meet your deadlines?** Many people can, on a moment's notice, provide a long list of things that affect their ability to meet their deadlines. Some are valid reasons; some are dog-ate-my-homework reasons. Listen for what they perceive as deadline disrupters, and you may learn about factors that could have a bearing on your success in meeting their expectations.

• **What departmental activities take too long?** Try to get a sense of how they interpret "too long" with regard to the activities they name. Find out how long they think these activities ought to take. This kind of question can give you insight into customers' expectations, especially if their responses pertain directly to your immediate work for the department. Like the preceding questions, this question can give you some sense of what customers view as reasonable or unreasonable.

• **What are the department's criteria for success?** In other words, what are the factors whose presence are critical to the success of the department and whose absence are an impediment to success? This question can help you understand what's most important to the department in general, and therefore what may be most important in seeking a solution to any specific service request. This question can provide a fascinating focus for discussion, because the customer department itself may never have thought about its responsibilities from this perspective.

In addition to generating useful information, questions such as these help you strengthen your relationship with your customers. People often complain about the idiosyncrasies, peculiarities, and unpredictabilities of their work, but rarely does anyone invite them to talk about it. So when you ask, it's likely you'll get an earful. In the process, these questions will enable you to develop a perspective of the goings-on in the department above and beyond anything you'd ever learn by focusing on immediate needs.

GATHER INFORMATION REGULARLY

As suggested earlier, you can add your own questions to those listed in this chapter. By having a list of questions to work from, you'll bring consistency to your information-gathering efforts and in the process generate more useful information.

But don't confine your information gathering to situations in which you are addressing specific problems. Periodically, supplement problem-specific sessions with general information-gathering meetings. These meetings should be for the sole purpose of improving your understanding of your customers and their work. The more you learn, the more proficient you'll be at understanding current expectations and anticipating future expectations. In the process, you'll build rapport that will help you and your customers better meet each other's expectations over the long term.

These meetings provide the opportunity to learn more about your customers than you can reasonably learn in the midst of a specific problem-solving situation. After all, when someone calls the help desk in a state of panic, it's probably not the best time to ask, "What factors affect your priorities, make you less efficient than you like, and make it difficult to meet your deadlines?" Do so, and you'll find that the answer, in one word, is "You!"

NOTES

[1] Donald C. Gause and Gerald M. Weinberg, *Are Your Lights On?* (New York: Dorset House Publishing, 1990), p. 54.

[2] Edward de Bono, *de Bono's Thinking Course* (New York: Facts on File, 1982), p. 74.

[3] DeMarco and Lister observe how easy it is to spend "too much of our time trying to get things done and not nearly enough time asking the key question, 'Ought this thing to be done at all?'" Tom DeMarco and Timothy Lister, *Peopleware* (New York: Dorset House Publishing, 1987), p. 11.

Hammer and Champy point out that the most impressive companies they examined were those that asked, not "How can we do what we do better?" but "Why do we do what we do at all?" Michael Hammer and James Champy, *Reengineering the Corporation* (New York: HarperCollins Publishers, 1993), p. 4.

[4] Gause and Weinberg, op. cit. p. 7.

8

Try the Solution On for Size
Why the specification is not the solution

When I went shopping for a new ski jacket, I learned how easy it is to misjudge solution specifications. The jacket I had no longer served my most important need: keeping warm.

Fortunately, I knew exactly what I wanted. My new jacket should be longer, to insulate me in single-digit temperatures. It should have a hood, to protect me from weather that makes the wind in my hair less than romantic. It should have lots of pockets. And it should be a bright color. I've always bought brightly colored ski jackets, so that was a must.

After trying on several jackets, I selected one that met all my specifications: It was long, thickly lined, full of pockets, had a hood, and was a bright color. A very bright color, actually. Iridescent orange. With this jacket, you'd be able to see me from the other side of the mountain, at night! I had found the perfect jacket.

FINDING THE PERFECT SOLUTION

When I got home, I put the jacket on and did my imitation of an Olympic racer.

Something was not quite right. I waited awhile and tried it on again. And then again. By the fifteenth time, I hated the jacket. Everything about it was wrong. It wasn't just long; it was too long. It wasn't just thickly lined—it made me look like a blimp. And the color. I'd not only be visible in total darkness, I'd also be visible to other skiers every time I fell. I don't fall often, but when I assume a horizontal orientation, I don't want the world to be my witness.

This jacket met my specs, yet it was all wrong. I grudgingly conceded that my solution wasn't perfect, and consoled myself that at least I found out before my next ski trip.

I returned the jacket and resumed my search. Another jacket caught my eye. I put it on. It was love at first sight. This jacket was lightweight, hoodless, and blue. Not bright blue, just blue. It met almost none of my specs. It wouldn't even meet my number one requirement, warmth, but I didn't care. It was roomy enough so I could wear extra sweaters. I scrapped my specs and bought the jacket.

This experience reminded me that specifications don't necessarily mean a thing. They're a good first approximation, based on everything customers know when they prepare them. They provide a focal point for saying "That's not it," but it's impossible to really know how well the solution will work in meeting expectations until you try it out in real circumstances, or at least in circumstances as close to real as possible. Maybe posing in my orange jacket at home wasn't as real as skiing in it, but it was close enough to make its flaws blatantly apparent.

BECOMING IMMERSED IN THE SOLUTION

Unfortunately, until customers have had a chance to live with a solution, they have no way of being sure it will meet their needs. They may assume the new solution will be effective simply because it's unlike the current one. Unfortunately, even if you are convinced that your customers' selected solution will not meet their needs, it is rarely effective to try to get them to change their minds. Instead, you must use methods that help them independently acquire a perspective of the solution that is closer to one you favor, so that they reach similar conclusions.

How can you accomplish this? In Chapter 5, we saw how prototypes can assist customers in finding a consensus during requirements analysis. Prototypes can also help in assessing a proposed solution. Usability labs are on the right track in creating simulated environments in which users can test prototypes and early versions of products in settings that approximate their own. With or without usability labs, what's important is to do as much prototyping as possible early in the project, even if it revolves around only very scaled-down elements of the final solution. Better to simulate only thirty percent of the functionality of the final product—and reveal flaws in the design—than to await the full solution and discover, too late, that it's seriously deficient.

If your organization doesn't have a usability lab, the following approaches can help customers broaden their perspective of solutions in such a way that they "own" their conclusions, rather than feel that decisions have been foisted on them.

Conduct a Demonstration

It's wise to demonstrate elements of a solution to customers as early in a project as you can. I witnessed a situation in which a complex third-party system was being customized to support the needs of a city agency. As soon as a skeleton of the system was installed, a high-level official, who would be one of its key users, was invited to see a demo. After a mere thirty seconds, his eyes lit up.

Suddenly, he was full of questions. Will the system do this? Can it handle that? Will it enable us to . . .? What if we . . . ? He didn't know that the demo database contained only a handful of records, nor did he know that only a fraction of the functionality was in place. It didn't matter. What mattered was that by seeing a portion of the system's capabilities firsthand, he was immediately able to envision the possibilities. He could ask questions that were far more on target than if he had been invited early on to specify his requirements.

"Could he have specified his requirements?" I asked the systems staff. Not a chance, they all agreed, not in a way that would have been precise enough or thorough enough. This demo proved to be a win-win expectations-managing device, which offered greater insight into his needs and priorities than any amount of interrogation could have.

What the city official was really doing was something pretty close to reviewing a chart with luggage photos and being asked to identify how his differed from the one most like his. He was able to observe system capabilities and appreciate immediately how they would support his needs. He was also able to ask intelligent questions about whether and how the system would accommodate other needs. Having something real to look at helped him understand his own requirements in a way he never could have in the abstract. It gave him something to look at and say "That's not it." He didn't say that, though, because he loved the system. What he said repeatedly, as the various capabilities were displayed, was "Wow!" The system met expectations he didn't even realize he had.

Facilitate a Solution Review

Solution reviews can help identify the flaws and weaknesses in a proposed solution before you've invested too much effort in it. In general, reviews can provide a forum for technical staff and customers to evaluate just about anything, such as a design, a specification, a strategy, a set of requirements, or, as in this case, a proposed solution. It's the rare review in which the product or process under review isn't improved through discussion by individuals with a range of backgrounds and expertise.[1]

Whether or not you conduct a formal solution review, periodic quick reviews can offer helpful feedback about solutions, both when they're first proposed and as they are under development. Bouncing your ideas off anyone else (or having your customer do so) is valuable, because feedback from others can raise questions and offer perspectives you might overlook otherwise. In fact, as mentioned in the previous chapter, those with the least familiarity with your problem often offer the best insights, because these individuals are not blocked by well-entrenched ideas.

However you conduct a solution review, what's important is that it is not treated as a fault-finding session, but rather that it serve as an opportunity for all parties to share ideas and challenge each other to devise the best possible solution.

Do a Plus/Minus Exercise

A solution review may be overkill for small solutions, especially if it would require more time than is needed to develop the solution itself. A plus/minus exercise may be more appropriate; it can be conducted as part of a formal solution review, or completely independent of one, and is extremely effective in assessing the quality of a proposed solution, regardless of size.

Edward de Bono—creator of the CAF technique we reviewed in Chapter 7—has an exercise called PMI, which stands for Plus Minus Interesting.[2] In this exercise, a group of people first spend about a minute identifying the pluses about a given issue, then a minute identifying the minuses, and finally a minute identifying aspects that are neither plus nor minus, but simply interesting. As de Bono suggests, one of the problems with thinking is that we tend to use it too much to back up opinions we've already formed, rather than to consider other perspectives. The PMI is a powerful technique, which results in those strongly in favor of an issue becoming aware of the pitfalls, and vice versa. And as de Bono points out, once you think something new on an issue, you can't unthink it.

I use variations of de Bono's PMI to help groups explore both sides of a solution. In one version, small groups spend five minutes identifying all the good aspects of a particular solution, then five minutes identifying all the not-so-good aspects. Alternatively, first ten good aspects are identified, then ten not-so-goods. The good and not-so-good segments of the exercise are deliberately kept separate to ensure that participants focus all attention on that aspect of it for a concentrated, although brief, period of time. In presenting this exercise to groups, I refer to the negative side as "not so good," rather than "bad," to foster a constructive mindset rather than a fault-finding one. What often happens is that those who have previously seen only the virtues or the flaws of a particular solution start to see the other side, thereby broadening their perspective. The aspects identified can then be the subject of additional analysis or discussion, if appropriate.

When I ran this exercise with one particular group, a participant commented that the solution under consideration was similar to one that had been tried before and failed. Interestingly, this participant viewed the previous failure as a not-so-good, because it suggested to him the solution was faulty; others in the group, however, viewed it as a good, because the group could learn from the failure in order to make the new solution succeed. It is not unusual for numerous responses to be seen as good by some participants and not-so-good by others in the same group.

This exercise has great value when conducted in groups of four to six individuals. The rapid exchange of ideas raises perspectives that any individual in the group might otherwise overlook, and invariably generates both pluses and minuses that no one considered initially. Furthermore, this exercise can be conducted among groups consisting only of your coworkers or colleagues, only your customers, or groups of both. The combined grouping can be the most valuable, because it enables the two groups to interact as a team with a common goal.

When group sizes permit, the exercise can also be structured as a friendly competition to see who identifies the most pluses and minuses in the allotted time. I've used this type of exercise to facilitate relationship-building between customers and technical staff, since it provides an opportunity for the members of the two groups to function as a team and, in the process, share views on a subject they might not otherwise have the occasion to discuss.

No matter what the mix of participants in these small groups, the resulting responses are often quite similar from one group to another. Participants who have previously focused on their differences are often surprised to discover they share many more views than they had previously appreciated. In the process, the solution or idea under review gets a surprisingly detailed assessment in a minimum amount of time.

Perform a Solution Analysis

A solution analysis considers both the good and the not-so-good aspects of a proposed solution, but it does so by focusing on a specific set of questions designed to help evaluate a proposed solution. The objective of a solution analysis is to raise questions to ensure that you think adequately about the ramifications—both positive and negative—of either a particular solution or the tradeoffs among alternative solutions.

Questions that focus on the positive ramifications concern the positive outcomes of a particular solution. For example,

- What will the solution allow us to do faster, cheaper, easier, or better?

- What factors make this solution attractive?

- What makes this the right time to implement this solution?

- How might the solution generate benefits that can't be fully foreseen?

- How is the solution similar to past endeavors that yielded broader benefits than expected?

- In what ways might the solution set the stage for efforts that might not otherwise be possible?

Questions that focus on the negative ramifications can help you identify factors that could prevent the success of a particular solution. For example,

- How might the solution demand more than meets the eye?

- How might the solution have a negative impact on resources?

- What unforeseen consequences might this solution create?

- What kinds of expectations might this solution create that could become difficult to satisfy?

- What new problems might this project or solution create?

You can then evaluate both positive and negative ramifications, and ask

- What aspects of the solution as initially envisioned now appear to be more important than we originally thought, and should be given particular attention?

- What aspects of the solution as initially envisioned now appear to contain flaws, and should be rethought?

- What other solutions should we consider?

- What can we now conclude about this proposed solution? Should we proceed with it?
  Should we modify it?

The preceding questions concern the impact of proceeding with a particular solution. A solution analysis should also consider the reverse side of the issue: What would be the impact of not implementing this solution—or any solution? For example, if you don't proceed with a particular solution,

- What will this organization or department not
  be able to accomplish?

- What competitive opportunities will be
  missed? What is the cost or impact of these
  missed opportunities?

- What future crises or obstacles might not be
  avoided?

- What other business efforts will become more
  complex, more expensive, or more involved as
  a result?

The final question for this analysis should be

- Before addressing this solution, what additional questions should we ask?

This last question often leads to others that might not have been considered, but that are worthy of attention. If so, address these questions, and then return to this one, repeating the process as many times as necessary until you can think of no additional questions you should ask.

This analysis can be performed individually or in groups, but may be most effective if you and your customers each start by sharing these questions with your respective coworkers, and then hold a group discussion. In fact, both this solution analysis and the questions in the previous chapter can have considerable educational value in helping customers more comprehensively consider their problems and proposed solutions before seeking your assistance. You might therefore find it helpful to compile a master list of questions for customer use, so they can do a more thorough job of assessing their needs before submitting a request to you.

Analyze What Can Go Wrong

The billing project described in Chapter 7 might have failed if it had been implemented. Many projects do go forward and do fail. For example, some years ago, travel authorities in a particular city decided to improve the frantic flow of rush-hour traffic by establishing the high-speed lane of an expressway as an express lane for use only by cars with three or more riders. Traffic crews set up dividers separating the high-speed lane from the other lanes, and designated a span of road just before the start of the dividers for switching into or out of the express lane. Clever, yes? No!

The express lane began just at the spot where two major highways merged. The resulting traffic jam caused by cars switching into and out of the express lane before reaching the dividers created traffic tie-ups unlike anything the city had ever seen. The solution was worse than the problem it tried to solve.

After months of pondering how to "fix the solution," traffic authorities finally decided to solve the new problem by eliminating it! No more express lane, no more dividers, just normal frantic rush-hour traffic. Driving into the city never seemed so easy.

Before proceeding with a solution, particularly if it will require a substantial investment in money or resources, be sure to ask: How might this solution fail? It can be a tough question to ask, especially if the solution is one you favor, but it is better to find out before it's too late. Before asking it, though, ask a related question: What constitutes failure?

You may find that you have one view and your customers have another. Is failure a solution that exceeds budget by one dollar or one million? Is it an implementation that takes place one day late or a year late? Is it a malfunction of some scope, an outage of some duration, or an inaccuracy of some proportion? Just as it's important to identify your customers' criteria for success, so that you know what will meet their expectations, it's important to know how they view failure, so that you know what will fail to meet their expectations.

Asking how the solution might fail may lead to the decision to abandon it, but it may also raise issues that improve the odds of implementing a good solution. That means that thinking about failure can make success even more likely. So be ruthless in asking this question, and tough-minded in answering it. It could be the most important question you ask.

Consider Alternative Solutions

In doing the previous analyses, you may conclude that your proposed solution is no longer the one you want, and you need to consider alternatives. But even if it remains the preferred solution, consider alternatives. In fact, try to come up with several. The very process of identifying other possible solutions, or even just variations on the preferred solution, may reveal issues that you would have overlooked otherwise. Then ask,

- What do these alternative solutions offer that the preferred solution doesn't? In what ways, if any, are they better solutions?

- What are the chief weaknesses of these other solutions? In what ways are they less effective solutions than the preferred one?

- What are the benefits of continuing with the preferred solution rather than switching to one of the alternatives? What are the pitfalls?

- What ideas do these alternative solutions raise that can be applied to the preferred solution?

Create Your Own Techniques

The techniques I've described are not the only options you have to help customers envision and evaluate solutions. Combine those in this chapter in various ways, or use your imagination and formulate your own.[3] For example,

- Evaluate the contribution of each feature to the overall solution, or question the impact on the solution if that feature were eliminated or changed in some way.

- Arrange visits to other sites to evaluate the solutions in use there. If you do so, be sure to include your customers in these visits. Work with customers to prepare a list of questions that will provide the basis for a review of demonstrations you will view or discussions you will hold. Afterward, schedule a discussion with your customers to compare your observations.

- Invite outsiders to participate in some of your internal demonstrations, evaluations, and discussions, either to bring an industry perspective or to describe their own experiences in dealing with similar solutions.

- Take the questions in Chapter 7, replace each occurrence of "problem" with "solution," and use the resulting questions to assess a proposed solution. This will focus attention on issues that may not get adequate coverage otherwise, such as the risks posed by the solution, and the impact of the solution on other business processes or other areas of your organization.

REFLECTING ON A JOB COMPLETED

Post-project reviews are a means of asking what you'd do differently if you knew before what you know now. They provide a structured way for you and your customers, either individually or jointly, to assess what worked well and what didn't. In other words, it's a process for reflecting on the process. A post-project review revolves around questions such as these:

- How well were responsibilities divided between customers and systems staff?

- How might responsibilities have been more effectively delegated?

- To what extent was the problem accurately identified?

- What sources of information and what questions that we asked initially were particularly helpful in understanding the problem?

- In what ways did the problem turn out to be something other than what it appeared?

- What additional sources of information or what questions might have led to a better understanding of the problem?

- What aspects of the solution turned out exactly as expected?

- What surprises emerged? How could they have been anticipated?

- What aspects of our interaction with each other worked well?

- What changes might have enabled the interaction to work better?

- What were the most important lessons learned in carrying out this effort?

- What should we do differently next time around?

To these questions, which are traditional post-project review questions, can be added specific expectations-oriented questions, such as, How well have we done in communicating our expectations to each other? and, How can we do better in the future? If problems have occurred, think about whether they may have been expectations-related.

Of course, in a well-managed project, you and your customers would continuously assess how well the effort is going, and make mid-course adjustments, as needed. The very process of regularly discussing how well you're doing in meeting each other's expectations significantly increases the likelihood that your solution will succeed.

A JACKET ANALYSIS

Systems solutions are unlike jacket solutions in one essential way. When I didn't like my orange jacket, I simply returned it for a full refund. Unless that's an option you offer your customers, you may want to try the techniques in this chapter to help both yourself and your customers gain a better idea of the suitability of a proposed solution. Doing so will improve the odds that, when you deliver the solution, their reaction will be the same as mine was when I found my blue jacket: "That's it!"

NOTES

[1]For a more detailed treatment of the subject of technical reviews, see Daniel P. Freedman and Gerald M. Weinberg, *Handbook of Walkthroughs, Inspections, and Technical Reviews,* 3rd. ed. (New York: Dorset House Publishing, 1990).

[2]Edward de Bono, *de Bono's Thinking Course* (New York: Facts on File, 1985), pp. 11-19.

[3]For other techniques and hints, see Donald C. Gause and Gerald M. Weinberg, *Exploring Requirements* (New York: Dorset House Publishing, 1989).

SECTION 3
Policies and Practices

Communication and information-gathering know-how will help you manage expectations on a case-by-case basis. However, on an organizational level, something more is needed: an infrastructure that facilitates managing expectations consistently and over the long term. This third section concerns the policies and practices that constitute that infrastructure, with emphasis on clarifying customer perceptions of your services, establishing service standards, creating reasonable boundaries on your workload, and most important of all, building strong relationships with customers. These policies and practices will help you and your customers create a shared understanding of what you can each reasonably and realistically expect from the other.

Guidelines 9 through 12 will enable you to

9. Clarify customer perceptions.

10. Set uncertainty-managing service standards.

11. When appropriate, just say whoa.

12. Build win-win relationships.

9

Clarify Customer Perceptions
Believing is seeing

Perception is reality. True or false? When I pose this question to groups I work with, it always generates a lively discussion: about the room being warm to one person and cool to another, for example, or about a turtle appearing to move slowly to a rabbit and quickly to a snail. The point is quickly made: It is easy for two observers to perceive the same thing differently.[1]

A perfect example of such differences concerns your services. The way your customers perceive your services may not match the way you perceive them—or want them perceived. Yet, their perception translates into the requests and demands they make of you. And it's this view that often creates the expectations you consider unreasonable. It's a circular process: Customers' perceptions influence their expectations of you, and their expectations, in turn, influence how they interpret what they perceive.[2]

Few organizations do enough to identify and clarify their customers' perceptions of their services. Yet, no matter what other steps you take to manage expectations, your efforts will fall short unless you address this issue of perceptions.

DIFFERING PERCEPTIONS

People's perceptions may differ even when they work closely or interact frequently. Therefore, if you find yourself thinking, "After all this time, they *must* understand," you may be making a mistake.

One of my most revealing personal experiences with differences in perceptions occurred when Howard and I were driving to a ski area in western Canada. As we neared the ski area, a sign outside a motel caught my eye: SAUNA. The motel looked somewhat run-down, but saunas are a rare treat for us, so Howard offered to go in and take a look. I said, "Fine. If it's OK with you, it's OK with me."

When Howard returned, he reported that the place looked fine and that he'd checked us in for a week's stay. We unloaded our ski gear and went to our room.

What a shock!

It was a cubbyhole. The bed was close to the floor. Correction: Parts of the bed were close to the floor. The mattress gave new meaning to the word undulating. The dresser must have been from the Nothing-Over-One-Dollar emporium (when I opened the drawers, they jammed and the knobs fell off). The room had only one dim bulb. The shower . . . well, you get the idea.

I was upset, but it was my own fault. I hadn't told Howard what I considered important. I'd said, "If it's OK with you, it's OK with me." At least it had a sauna.

We went to check it out. The sign on the sauna door said: OUT OF ORDER. That's when I lost my temper. Howard should have known I would hate this place.

Or should he have?

We decided to leave. ("We came here for the sauna," we complained. Talk about creating false expectations!) The manager ripped up our credit-card slip, eager to see us leave before we discouraged other guests who also might like their saunas hot.

A mile up the road, we found a very nice condo apartment. This time, we made sure we'd *both* be happy with it. I had learned a lesson. The question is, Why did this situation occur? At first glance, the problem may appear to be that Howard's perception of motel comfort differed from mine. But that wasn't really the problem, because any two people's perceptions almost always differ. The problem was that we forgot that. And since I was the one who really cared in this instance, I should have made it my responsibility to compare our perceptions and to ensure they were sufficiently in sync.

PERFORMING FOR SATISFACTION

It's easy to conclude that customer satisfaction is determined by your performance, but it's not; it's determined by your customers' *perception* of your performance. The gap between how they view you and how you think they view you may be bigger than you realize, and it may require some concerted effort to narrow that gap.

How do you think your customers perceive your services? To most customers, your work is a mystery. They envision you spending your time hunched over a keyboard, "playing" with software, or doing something easy (in their eyes) like training or systems development, and these perceptions influence their attitude toward you. Most customers don't understand the nature, scope, or complexity of your work. Therefore, if they perceive that you deliver services A, B, and C, that's what they're going to expect of you, whether or not it's what you do. And if they perceive your work as simple, they will expect you to respond accordingly.

These perceptions are powerful: If customers perceive that you are slow, careless, or unreliable, then you *are* slow, careless, or unreliable in their eyes, and your attempts to persuade them otherwise may not sway their viewpoint. The reverse situation is also true: If you really are slow, careless, and unreliable but customers perceive that you're swift, accurate, and dependable, then you are, in their eyes.

Similarly, if customers perceive simple efforts as complex, they will respond accordingly. I experienced this firsthand when a politically important customer casually mentioned that she had a terrible time comparing data from multiple reports. We fixed her problem in five minutes. She, however, perceived it as a herculean effort and was ecstatic. We chose not to challenge that perception. As a rule, however, it's best not to assume perceptions will work in your favor this way.[3]

DISCUSSING CUSTOMER PERCEPTIONS

Before you know if you need to reorient customer perceptions, you have to know what those perceptions are. Lay the groundwork for finding out by discussing these perceptions with the members of your group. The outcome of such a discussion is a much clearer appreciation of how, for better or worse, you contribute to your customers' perceptions of you.

Questions About Perceptions

Here are some questions to drive your discussion:
• **How do you think customers perceive your services?** Of course, you can't speak for your customers, but discussing this issue can provide a basis for comparison with responses

derived from surveys and other methods, such as those described later in this chapter. Be aware that thinking about customers' perceptions may also raise some interesting issues about how you and members of your group perceive yourselves. Differences in perspective among management and staff, and among coworkers, on such issues as accessibility, flexibility, and service orientation are not unusual.

• **What types of customer expectations do you experience that you would characterize as unreasonable?** Identify some specific examples and describe why they are unreasonable. Explain why you think these expectations exist and what their impact is on you, your group, and the services you provide. Consider possible reasons the customer's action or attitude might not be unreasonable if viewed from that customer's perspective.

• **What are the likely consequences of customer perceptions that are less favorable than you'd like them to be?** Think about what your relationship with your customers will be like one year from now if you take no action to change these perceptions. Consider the impact on you, your department, your customers, and your organization. Describe the basis for your responses.

• **What do your responses lead you to conclude about customer perceptions?** Have your conclusions changed from what they were before this discussion? Many groups that hold this type of discussion reach a similar conclusion: Most of the customer expectations considered unreasonable are perfectly reasonable from the customer's perspective; and the key to bringing customer expectations closer to the group's is a clarification of what can realistically be accomplished.

Discussions of Perceptions: Two Examples

It's not unusual for discussions of customer perceptions to lead to improved strategies for managing expectations. Two groups' experiences illustrate this point. The first, a technical support group, had recently analyzed its call statistics and found that the number of calls for help with relatively simple problems was on the rise. Furthermore, a small number of problems accounted for a disproportionately large number of calls. This call analysis came up during a discussion of customer perceptions.

The group's initial reaction was that customers expected too much help to resolve problems they should have been able to handle themselves. However, as they thought about their customers' perspective, it became obvious that their own promotional material and their service motto of "Call us; we're here to help you" contributed to this phenomenon. They acknowledged that customers were not unreasonable to expect assistance for simple or repeat problems, since the support group had reinforced that expectation by readily accepting and acting on every call.

In thinking about the impact of this service orientation on their effectiveness, group members agreed that devoting so much time to simple or recurring problems diverted them from initiating more proactive support efforts. They concluded that before they could change their customers' perceptions and the resulting expectations, they would have to reorient both their services and their promotional strategies. By the end of the session, group members had generated a list of ways to promote increased customer self-sufficiency, and to provide better support before problems occurred.

What happened here is typical: A discussion of customer perceptions led to the identification of a much broader issue—the effectiveness of the group's service strategies—and the decision to address the issue.

The second example concerns an IS group whose customers occasionally asked for help in completing the justification section of their service requests. Group members said that, although requests for such justification assistance were infrequent, each such instance was a time-consuming interruption; they asserted that customers should be able to prepare their own justifications. But in discussing customer perceptions, group members conceded that it was not necessarily reasonable to expect customers to know how to justify computer services, and that guiding them in doing so would benefit both customers and themselves.

As a result, they decided to prepare guidelines to help customers perform their own justifications. Thinking about these guidelines led the group to outline what customers can do to better assess their needs before preparing a service request. This discussion led the group to realize that the service request itself was an expectations-managing form, and that it could include information that would help evaluate the request and manage the subsequent project.

Anticipate the Consequences of Discussion

Fair warning: As these examples demonstrate, discussing customer perceptions can open up a can of worms. Analyzing one problem leads quite naturally to analysis of others. Discussing one approach leads to discussion of others. And thinking about customer perceptions, particularly if you haven't done so before, may lead to a new assessment of your services. Unfortunately, much of what you decide you want to change won't change without effort. It takes work and may require numerous meetings, discussions, and negotiations with customers. But the improvements can more than compensate for the effort if they lead to more realistic customer perceptions.

GAINING FEEDBACK FROM CUSTOMERS

Since it's easy to misjudge how your customers perceive you, it's important to get feedback directly from them. Identifying customer perceptions is an information-gathering task that can be carried out in several ways, including surveys, individual or group interviews, and meetings with groups of customers.

Customer Surveys

The customer survey is the most common method of soliciting feedback. Unfortunately, surveys have become overused, and people are tired of being asked to fill them out. As one customer told me emphatically, "Whenever I get a survey form, I just toss it directly into the waste basket." Moreover, many of the surveys I've evaluated suffer from flaws in design, administration, and interpretation. For example, these surveys are rarely tested on prospective respondents to determine the clarity of the questions. Without understanding how customers interpret survey questions, it's impossible to know how to interpret the responses.

However, since no other method can provide as much feedback as quickly as a survey, the solution is not to eliminate them, but to take steps that will make it possible to use the results with confidence in drawing conclusions about customer perceptions. For example,

• **Specify exactly what issues require feedback.** Asking vague questions about how customers perceive your services or your department will generate similarly vague, and therefore useless, responses. Focus on specifics, such as how customers perceive your responsiveness in solving technical problems, or how they perceive your flexibility in adjusting to their changing priorities.

• **Request specific examples that illustrate responses.** Rankings alone are easy to misinterpret; what one person means by a rating of six on a seven-point scale isn't necessarily the same as what another person means.

• **Provide plenty of space for written explanations.** You will receive considerably more written feedback by doing so than if you provide little or no space.

• **Keep the survey as brief as possible.** Surveys that can be completed in ten minutes are more likely to be filled out than those requiring thirty minutes. Test the timing on members of your own group as well as on selected customers. State the approximate completion time in bold type at the start of the survey.

• **Provide a due date.** Omitting a date guarantees that many customers will add the survey to their "later" pile, from which it may never emerge. Sending out a reminder as the due date approaches increases the number of responses.

• **Consider requesting signatures.** Since some customers will not respond if signatures are required, consider making signatures optional but strongly encourage customers to sign their surveys. Having respondents' signatures will enable you to get additional information about their concerns.

• **Announce your plans to conduct a survey.** Don't spring it on customers without warning. Describe its importance to you, and let them know how you intend to use it.

• **Test the survey on a small group of customers.** Ask test-group members to explain how they interpret your questions. Have them identify any ambiguous or unclear wording. Invite their suggestions about ways to generate a high response rate. Request their assistance in encouraging their own coworkers to complete the survey.

One-on-One Interviews

An alternative to using surveys is to meet one-on-one with selected customers. The number of such interviews depends on the size and functional distribution of the customer community. I've found that about a dozen interviews, with customers from management and non-management levels throughout the organization, generates a solid base of information about perceptions.

At these interviews, ask customers to describe their experiences in working with your group. Request their comments in terms of specific criteria, such as accessibility or cooperativeness. As with surveys, request concrete examples to illustrate their comments. Determine if they are unaware of services that are currently available. Also ask if they have encountered services elsewhere that would be helpful to them if incorporated into your services. Have them describe services or assistance they've been pleased with, as well as problems they've experienced.

Keep your questions open-ended. This is not the place for multiple-choice questions that will provide clues about what the "right" answers are. Take copious notes for later review, and, if possible, work with a partner so that one of you can lead the discussion while the other takes notes.

Team Interviews

You might also join forces with customers to conduct interviews in pairs, each pair consisting of one member of your group and one customer. In working with you, these customers serve as members of your perception-management team. This method is not used often, but it can be very effective; it's difficult for customers to be totally objective about the responses they elicit from their coworkers, but it is just as difficult for you to be completely objective about customers' comments. The team approach provides a basis for subsequent comparison of views and formation of conclusions.

In conducting customer interviews with members of client organizations, I have found that, as an outside consultant, I can be more objective in listening to customer feedback than my clients. On the other hand, they have a much broader appreciation of the history and context of the relationships with customers, which is valuable in interpreting the resulting feedback.

Customer-Led Interviews

Another approach to interviewing is to have customers conduct one-on-one interviews with members of their own business units. A common apprehension about this approach is that customers will not be objective in seeking feedback from their peers. This is a reasonable concern; however, when such customers are officially designated participants on an evaluation team, and the team has been designed so that all participants have a stake in improving their relationship with each other, customers will carry out interviews in a professional and reasonably objective manner. Their goal, after all, is to help communicate their perspective about what is working and what's not.

The risk of subjectivity in this type of situation is balanced by the opportunity it provides for one-on-one feedback from many more customers than would otherwise be possible. Customer-led interviews also make it possible to gain feedback from customers at remote sites who may have strong views about the support they receive, but who might otherwise be omitted from the perception-checking process.

Group Meetings

Another way to learn about customer perceptions that generates considerable feedback, and invariably a few surprises, is to hold meetings with up to a dozen customers, and to discuss their perceptions as a unit. Many such customers have not previously had the opportunity to compare views on the services they've received, and the synergy that results leads to more wide-ranging feedback than is generated from a survey or interview. I've observed IS staff at such meetings scratch their heads in response to comments from customers, and I know that these head-scratchings mean, "How could they be so far off base in their understanding of what we do?" Their question might more appropriately be, "How could we be so far off base as not to have identified these perceptions sooner and done something to rectify them?"

Not that all customers share identical views—it is not uncommon for some customers to express satisfaction and others to express dissatisfaction with the same aspects of your performance. In a well-facilitated meeting, customers can discuss their viewpoints constructively, providing you with insight into the diversity of their perceptions. You are then better prepared to consider what changes should be made.

Your Participation

Before deciding which of these several approaches to use, consider the pros and cons of your own participation. If you take part, you'll hear customer comments firsthand, which will be more enlightening, for example, than a summary from a customer-led interview. Furthermore, your participation can help strengthen your relationship with customers, because the very process of a dialogue helps to improve your understanding of each other.

However, your presence might inhibit open discussion, and customer reluctance to express dissatisfaction could reduce the value of the meeting. Although many systems people predict their customers will overwhelm them with complaints, many customers are uncomfortable about voicing their dissatisfaction and require some gentle coaxing. The presence of the person whose services they want to complain about could prevent them from doing so.

It may not be easy to ask customers about their perceptions of you, but doing so doesn't have to be a heart-stopping challenge. Once you've obtained their feedback, avoid the temptation to become defensive about perceptions you consider negative. Instead, view your findings as valuable data that can help you bring their perceptions more in line with your reality.

CREATING A SERVICE GUIDE

One of the common conclusions from customer feedback is that customers need better information about the services available to them. However, providing this information isn't as easy as saying, "We design databases," "We provide technical support," or "We conduct training." It's important to use all available outlets to communicate services.

Presentations, meetings with customers, and newsletters all provide effective ways to communicate service information, but a service guide can provide the most comprehensive picture of your services. Effective service guides should contain a mission statement, ground rules for providing services, constraints in delivering them, methods for setting priorities, service request procedures, and itemization of customer responsibilities.

It's also important to specify what services you don't provide. Customers may think that you perform some service or task, either because you have done so or have led them to believe that you've done so. So if you don't install networks, develop applications, or change passwords, but customers persistently request such assistance, state clearly that you don't. If you can identify people in or outside your organization who can help customers with these efforts, or ways they can help themselves, all the better.

Statement of Benefits

One additional category of information important in a service guide is a statement of the benefits of your services. Don't assume that benefits are obvious to customers; state them in business terms, such as cost or time savings, improved efficiency, increased productivity, access to critical information, or whatever else customers will be able to do better, faster, or differently as a result of your services.

By including a statement of benefits, a service guide can serve as a marketing tool. Marketing your services is an important part of your job, whether or not you charge for these services, and the guide may not have the intended marketing impact unless customers understand how they can benefit by using your services. Most customers who used to be totally dependent on your services now have a range of alternatives they can consider, making information about benefits particularly important for competitive reasons. Preparing an annual report that summarizes for customers the projects completed or services delivered in the past year, along with the benefits achieved or anticipated, can reinforce the information in the service guide.

Image Enhancement

In addition to its value in clarifying customer perceptions and marketing your services, a service guide can substantially enhance your image with customers. For example, one customer support group was concerned because customers had only a limited idea of the scope of its services. The group prepared a comprehensive, beautifully designed service guide, distributed it, and was overwhelmed with positive feedback from customers who commented, "I didn't know you do so much." The document increased customer respect and broadened awareness when customers saw the range of services the group provided.

Do you risk creating new expectations in disseminating information that broadens your customers' view of your services? Absolutely, but by documenting your ground rules, constraints, priority-setting methods, and customer responsibilities, you will be creating realistic expectations, not runaway demands.

Clarifying Your Own Perceptions

A service guide helps clarify customer perceptions; it also forces you to clarify your own perceptions of your services. Customers may be confused about what to expect if different members of your own group give out different signals.

For example, in many end-user computing support groups, staff members view one of their most important goals as promoting customer self-sufficiency; yet each staff member may define self-sufficiency differently, and may promote it in a manner that contradicts other definitions. In such a case, it isn't surprising that customers are unclear about these services. It's important to identify conflicting views among departmental staff about services provided to customers, and to achieve a consensus before communicating information to customers.

EXPLAINING YOUR DECISIONS

Perception management involves more than just producing a service guide. When customers have not been told the reasoning behind decisions that have a direct impact on them, these decisions may appear arbitrary. From the customers' vantage point, the decisions may seem to impede their productivity. Customers' resentment about changes they don't understand may lead to refusal to follow standards.

Why As Well As What

When such negative reactions occur, the question to ask yourself is, "Have I adequately explained the why behind the what?" Often, providing an explanation not only prevents a negative reaction, but also increases customer support. In fact, keeping customers informed can help foster win-win relationships, even when you have to eliminate services.

For example, a help desk group was planning to reduce its support hours due to staff cutbacks and feared a backlash when customers learned about it. To avert such a reaction, they met with customer representatives and explained the reason for their decision. They also discussed support alternatives and ensured customers they'd still provide support in the event of off-hour emergencies. Because this group let customers know what to expect, a negative reaction never materialized. Customers would have preferred to keep things as they were, but they accepted the new restrictions and in the process became more self-sufficient.

Advance Notice

Be careful that you inform customers about planned changes far enough in advance. Don't surprise them with a sudden "We don't do that any more!" Giving them advance notice is a basic courtesy. But it's more than that; sometimes, failing to inform customers in advance can create new problems that are just as bad as the old problems.

I saw this happen in a company in which systems management decided that new systems would no longer include report programs. Instead, they reasoned, customers could use reporting tools to generate their own reports, and thereby save the systems staff considerable time. Unfortunately, no one informed customers of this new policy. As a result, the first such system developed under the new policy failed to take into account crucial database-design considerations and data format requirements necessary to support the customers' data access needs. The result? To generate their own reports, customers needed so much systems support that it more than offset the time savings management had anticipated.

Management Rationale

Systems staff, too, need to understand the why behind the what; yet, in the name of customer service, systems managers sometimes take action that, in the absence of an explanation, appears arbitrary, if not downright bizarre. This was the experience of an IS group whose director compressed the selection of a customer support system into an unreasonably short time. The group would have preferred more time to analyze the choices and more involvement in the ultimate selection.

When the director realized the intensity of staff discomfort with her approach, she explained that many customers were extremely dissatisfied with IS services and told her so daily. Consequently, she felt under extreme pressure to take action that would help address the situation. Since each member of the IS division experienced only a small fraction of this customer dissatisfaction, few had any appreciation of the scope of the problem. The director's after-the-fact explanation did not make her decision-making style more palatable to staff, but it did help them understand the reason for her actions and provided a basis for discussing how future decisions might be better communicated.

INVOLVING CUSTOMERS

One of the best ways to improve your customers' perception of your services and to help them achieve more realistic expectations is to involve them in your efforts. I discovered the value of customer involvement when I was in charge of a mammoth daily production system in which minor changes predictably caused unpredictable things to happen.

Acceptance Testing Teams

On one particular occasion, we were making a critical and complex series of modifications to the system. To ensure adequate testing, we asked the customer manager to select some members of his department to serve as an acceptance testing team, and to send them to work in our department for the duration of the testing effort. Day one of acceptance testing arrived, and in walked the team selected for the task. It was clear from their attitude they wanted nothing to do with us. They'd do their job and be done with it. "Six weeks," they said, and they'd be gone.

Six months later, they were still with us. No, not because their projected six weeks of work took six months—it took three months—but the testing process worked so well that it wasn't disbanded at the end of the original test cycle. Instead, the team was assigned another set of changes to test, and then another. Finally, the acceptance testing team was formalized as a permanent team that reported to business management, but resided in our department and worked side by side with us.

What happened during the initial testing cycle was that our customers got a strong dose of the reality of doing systems work. They learned, firsthand, about designing transactions, running tests, dealing with malfunctions, and waiting for hardware outages to end. Although they didn't do any genuinely technical work, their proximity to our technical work had a huge impact on them. By observing us pulling our hair out while we debugged the errors they detected, they began to appreciate what our verbal explanations never succeeded in communicating: Systems work is complex and can't necessarily be done as quickly as customers would like.

The most valuable outcome of this experience was one we didn't anticipate: These customers became our mouthpiece to the rest of the organization. They showed up full of animosity toward us, yet by a month later they had become our strongest supporters. Previously, when we had tried to explain the intricacies of their requests, their management thought we were simply making excuses. Now, the acceptance testing team rose to our defense, and told their superiors, "Wait a minute, you don't appreciate what's involved."

It was almost comical; they began to sound *just like us*. The difference, though, was that now their management listened, and heard. We had become credible to customer management in a way we never would have on our own. And because their perceptions more closely matched our reality, their expectations of us became more reasonable.

INTERPRETING COMPLAINTS

It is not enough to clarify perceptions once and assume that what you learn will suffice from that point forward. This issue always comes to mind when systems staff tell me things are going well. When I ask them how they can be sure, sometimes they report that their customers aren't complaining. "If there were any problems, we'd hear from them," they tell me.

Using an absence of complaints as a measure of customer satisfaction can be risky. Worse, it can be a fatal mistake, especially if you offer services that are also available from competitors. Instead of indicating that "all is well," the silence could mean that customers have become too discouraged to voice their complaints.

The absence of complaints could also mean something worse, as one systems group learned, too late, when a major customer department decided to obtain the same services from an outside firm. The switch was made for the most obvious of reasons: a better price. The department manager was a longtime IS customer who had been happy with the services provided, but who responded to budget cuts by selecting an outside vendor—and never mentioned a word to the systems group until the deed was done.

It's impossible to say whether this group could have retained the business if they had known the customers' concerns. The point is that they didn't—and by the time they did, it was too late.

Checkpoint Assessments

Clearly, it's as important to reassess your customers' perceptions when things are going well as when they aren't. Checkpoint assessments provide a systematic opportunity, a few times a year, to determine whether you and your customers are still in sync. Whether conducted by survey, interview, discussion, or any other form, such assessments are a chance to ask

- Have your expectations of our services changed?

- Do our products and services still meet your needs?

- Are you satisfied with the way we are serving you?

- Has anything happened that we should know about?

In conducting a checkpoint assessment, you invite customers to examine their changes in perspective. You can make these assessments even more effective by informing customers of the process in advance, and by identifying the concerns you will pursue. That way, customers will be better prepared to inform you of changes they might otherwise fail to mention.

Assure customers, though, that they don't have to wait until a scheduled assessment to voice their concerns; in fact, designate a specific individual who can serve in an ombudsman role, someone they can contact at any time. By providing an official outlet for their grievances, you assure them that their concerns are not only important, but welcome. You are therefore more likely to be in a position to act on their problems before it's too late. The role of this expectations manager will be discussed in the final chapter.

SAUNAFACTION GUARANTEED

Clarifying perceptions can be well worth the effort, whether you're delivering systems services or looking for motel accommodations while on a ski trip. Did I mention that the condo apartment Howard and I took for the week had its own private sauna? And it worked, too.

NOTES

[1]Joel Barker's view is that we literally see the world through our paradigms, which act as physiological filters. He states that any data that "exists in the real world that does not fit your paradigm will have a difficult time getting through your filters." Joel Arthur Barker, *Paradigms: The Business of Discovering the Future* (New York: HarperCollins, 1993), p. 86. Barker also cites Thomas S. Kuhn (*The Structure of Scientific Revolutions*, Chicago: University of Chicago Press, 1970, p. 150), who pointed out that even scientists can see the same thing differently. According to Kuhn, two groups of scientists who practice in different disciplines "see different things when they look from the same point in the same direction. Again, that is not to say they can see anything they please. Both are looking at the world, and what they look at has not changed. But, in some areas, they see different things, and they see them in different relations one to the other."

[2]For more on the impact of perceptions, see Thomas Gilovich, *How We Know What Isn't So* (New York: The Free Press, 1991).

[3]According to Robert Cialdini, there is a principle in human perception, the contrast principle, that affects the way we see the difference between two things that are presented one after another. According to this principle, "if the second item is fairly different from the first, we will tend to see it as more different than it actually is. So if we lift a light object first and then lift a heavy object, we will estimate the second object to be heavier than if we had lifted it without first lifting the light one." Robert A. Cialdini, *Influence: Science and Practice* (Glenview, Ill.: Scott, Foresman and Co., 1985), p.12. From this principle, we might speculate that if your

customers perceive you as swift, and you subsequently act in a manner they regard as slow, they might see you as even slower, by contrast, than you really are, and vice versa. In practice, however, when people become accustomed to a certain level of performance, it often takes more than a single contrasting experience before their expectations shift toward the new level.

10

Set Uncertainty-Managing Service Standards

Respect your customers' wait state

Often, the hardest thing for customers to cope with is not knowing what to expect. Even when you are hard at work doing exactly what you promised, customers wonder, Did they get my message? When will they get back to me? When will my problem be fixed? How long do I have to wait?

Recognizing how unsettling this type of uncertainty is for customers, and taking action to reduce it, are important elements of managing expectations. Just knowing how long they will have to wait for some anticipated action to take place, such as the arrival of someone who can help, is sometimes more important to customers than whether that duration is desirable or convenient. Not knowing what to expect makes the situation extremely stressful, and is a leading cause of customer dissatisfaction. That's why the establishment of service standards that tell customers what they can expect will prevent or reduce customer anxiety.

Chapter 9 offered ways of using a service guide to communicate to customers. This chapter's guideline describes several types of service standards and presents issues to consider in establishing them.

STANDARDS FOR COMMUNICATING "WHEN"

The impact of service standards struck me during a skiing experience in Vermont a few years ago. Actually, it was a non-ski experience. Howard and I were in line for a chair lift when it was shut down for repairs.

When I asked one of the lift operators how long the repair would take, he said it would require about forty-five minutes. Just enough time for a lunch break, we decided.

This estimate was important because it communicated more than a length of time. It also told us that the shutdown wasn't due to a complex problem. Most likely, it was a minor repair which, if made now, would prevent serious problems later. As the customer, I appreciated that; I once spent an hour in a stopped chair lift far above mother earth, and wholeheartedly preferred forty-five minutes off to another such hour on. Howard and I took off our gear, went into the lodge, and sat down for a quick lunch.

Thirty minutes later, eager to check on the progress of the repair, we bundled up again and went back to the lift area. We found that service had been restored, and the lift operators were once again sending skiers upward bound.

Clever folks, I remember thinking. They knew that if they told us thirty minutes to begin with, skiers would have begun lining up at the twenty-five-minute mark, eager to be whisked up into the frigid Vermont air. Instead, they astutely told us forty-five minutes to lower our expectations and give themselves some leeway.

What Your Service Philosophy Communicates

Advising customers how long they will have to wait communicates both a service standard and a service philosophy. As a service standard, the lift operator's forty-five minute estimate provided a period of time within which we could expect the repair to be completed. It gave us something to "know," instead of something to wonder about, and influenced our expectations about how long we'd have to wait.

This estimate also communicated the ski area's service philosophy that customers are entitled to know the status of services that affect them. But was this really their service philosophy? It wasn't until that evening, when I was comfortably ensconced in front of the roaring fire, that I realized I knew the estimate only because I asked. So perhaps the service philosophy was actually, "Tell 'em what you have to tell 'em, and if they don't ask, don't tell 'em."

What about your own service philosophy? Is it "We're here to serve you," or is it closer to "Go away, we're busy!"? Either is fine, provided you accept the impact of that philosophy on customer satisfaction. The problem is that sometimes an organization claims its philosophy is "We're here to serve you," while what its customers perceive is "Go away, we're busy!"

What Customers Can Expect

Service standards address this uncertainty by providing a formal method of letting customers know what they can expect. Service standards can be useful for a variety of services, such as problem acknowledgment, problem diagnosis and resolution, status updates, recovery assistance, and product support. The following are examples of service needs and sample service standards:

- **For routine services:** *We will provide customers with a daily update of all reported problems that remain unresolved.*

- **For activities that are part of a recurring process:** *We will acknowledge service requests within twenty-four hours of receipt, and provide written feedback on the action to be taken within one week of receipt.*

- **For activities that lead to repeated status requests:** *When hardware outages occur that will adversely affect the production schedule, we will issue a status update to the names on the Production Contact List every thirty minutes.*

- **For services that help promote sound computing practices:** *We will offer immediate data recovery support to customers who have performed backups, and twenty-four hour support to all other customers.*

- **For situations that result in what you perceive to be unreasonable expectations about your performance:** *We will address service requests in the priority sequence established by the Strategic Review Committee.*

- **For situations that can cause significant anxiety about the resumption of service after a departure from normal service:** *Replacement equipment will be provided within one hour for PC hardware malfunctions that cannot be corrected within that hour.*

In all these cases, service standards give customers information about "when" without their having to ask or wondering if you've forgotten them.

What You Expect of Customers

Service standards also provide a formal way to advise customers what you expect from them, so that you can best serve them. For example, in conjunction with your services, you may request that customers

- have a manual handy when they call you for help

- assign a project sponsor for any project that exceeds a certain scope or duration

- report on the benefits that have resulted within a specified period after a systems implementation

- keep you informed of all upcoming major projects in which they may need your assistance

These standards all help to communicate a division of responsibilities between you and your customers, so that you can meet each other's expectations.

CATEGORIES OF STANDARD-SETTING

Organizations typically fall along a standard-setting continuum that ranges from having no established standards to having formal, negotiated standards. Within this continuum are five categories of standard-setting:

1. No Standard-Setting

2. Internal Standard-Setting

3. Unilateral Standard-Setting

4. Standard-Setting with Feedback

5. Collaborative Standard-Setting

In reviewing these categories, consider which of the five most resembles your own organization. Then, think about the ways in which your organization differs from that one.

1. No Standard-Setting. Organizations that fall into this category do not have formally established service standards. Not surprisingly, these are the organizations that complain most often about customers having unreasonable expectations. Although such organizations lack formally stated standards, customers translate the services they receive into a level of expectation, and this becomes what they view as the service standard.

For example, customers who leave a voice-mail message for technical support, and get no response within what they consider a reasonable time, may perceive the organization's service standard to be inadequate. Similarly, service that consistently meets customers' needs is viewed as a standard, even if no such standard has been formally communicated. Therefore, although Category 1 organizations often think they have no service standards, customers perceive otherwise based on their own recent or recurring experiences with the organization.

2. Internal Standard-Setting. These organizations have service standards that they don't communicate to customers, but rather use for gauging organizational effectiveness and monitoring staff performance. For example, these organizations may set a time limit within which they intend to resolve technical problems or to respond to requests for assistance. Such standards serve an important internal expectations-managing function: They give service personnel targets to shoot for, while setting reasonable limits; and they provide a measure against which performance can be gauged. But these organizations don't publish standards for customers, often because they fear that doing so would prevent them from modifying their service strategies in response to changing workloads or resource constraints. As with Category 1 organizations, in the absence of formally communicated service standards, customers draw their own conclusions.

3. Unilateral Standard-Setting. Organizations in this category establish standards, document them, and communicate them to customers, but they don't solicit customer feedback regarding how well these standards meet their customers' needs. The standard-setting process is entirely a one-way process based on the organization's perception of customers' needs and their ability to respond to those needs. These standards may prove to be perfectly on target relative to customers' needs, or they may deviate significantly from those needs. In the absence of formally solicited customer feedback, it is difficult to know which is the case.

4. Standard-Setting with Feedback. These organizations establish, document, and publish their service standards. They also seek feedback from customers about the adequacy of these standards, and use this feedback to make adjustments to their services and service standards. The invitation to offer feedback communicates to customers that their views matter, an important aspect of relationship building. However, aside from providing feedback, customers are not otherwise involved in the standard-setting process.

5. Collaborative Standard-Setting. Although many people use the term "service agreement" when referring to Category 3 or 4, this fifth category is the only one that qualifies as a true service agreement: a two-way expectations-managing mechanism that results from a collaborative effort. Organizations that fall into Category 5 work closely with their customers to establish service standards that take into account customer needs as well as the organization's ability to respond to those needs. The standard-setting process entails a careful review of customers' goals and priorities, and identifies the responsibilities of both the customer and service provider in ensuring that the standards can be met. Moreover, it provides both formal and informal mechanisms for reviewing these standards and for periodically revising them, if needed, to eliminate service inadequacies or address changing business needs. If you suspect that such service agreements are rare, you are right.

Select the Category You Can Implement

Which category is the most appropriate for your organization and your services? It may seem that Category 5, Collaborative Standard-Setting, is the best, because it lets both you and your customers know what to expect. And that the fourth category is next best, and then the third, the second, and finally the first. But this is not necessarily the case, because the "best" category is whichever one you can implement and manage most successfully.

In determining which category will suit you, be aware that Category 5 is the most complex of the five, both to implement and manage. Implementation takes the greatest amount of effort, and may require numerous meetings and substantial negotiations with customers. Organizations eager to promote partnerships with their customers typically view Category 5 as the optimal approach, and indeed it can be. However, for many such organizations, the effort to implement a service agreement never moves beyond a statement of intent, either because they falter in selling the notion of such an agreement to customers or because participants in the effort become overwhelmed by the scope of the implementation task. Months later, after little or no progress, many organizations terminate their efforts to implement a service agreement.

Even though Categories 3 and 4 lack extensive customer involvement in the standard-setting process, a successfully implemented Category 3 or 4 approach will do far more to manage expectations than a Category 5 approach that fails.

Categories 1 and 2 should not be summarily dismissed as ineffective in managing expectations. Although these categories can contribute to unreasonable customer expectations, such expectations are not inevitable. That's because some organizations excel at providing high-quality services and keeping customers informed, even in the absence of formal service standards. Furthermore, their corporate culture may be one which fosters a more ad hoc, casual approach, and in which fewer standards are better than more.

Select the Category You Can Support

Especially important in determining the most appropriate category is your own ability to adhere to the standards you set. Standards that promise a level of service that you can't reliably provide are worse than no standards at all. For example, I once consulted with a company that was preparing to sell software support to corporate customers. To promote the service, the company was developing a marketing brochure which I was asked to review. The brochure contained this boldest-of-bold service standard: *We guarantee to solve all problems within one hour.* I tactfully suggested to my client that this claim might be just a bit risky, because a service organization's reputation is one of its most important products, and if it doesn't meet its own standards—and particularly those as easy to monitor as the minute hand on the clock—a positive reputation could quickly vanish.

My sinister side decided a test was called for, so I presented my client with a software problem, explaining it as it might have been stated by a confused novice. Find a solution? My client's technical staff couldn't even understand the problem; instead, they kept focusing on the problem they thought I was describing instead of the one I was describing in my deliberately muddled way. Partway through the hour, my client ripped up the proposed marketing brochure. It's a good thing, because if I'd been a genuine customer, I would have been intolerant of the company's inability to solve my problem within an hour. After all, they had guaranteed.

STRATEGIES FOR STANDARD-SETTING

In determining the advisability of service standards and the best approach to establishing them, assess the pros and cons of various approaches not in the abstract, but in the context of the benefits and risks relative to your particular environment. Following are some aspects of standard-setting worth consideration.

Service Targets

Instead of formulating service standards as guarantees, consider setting standards that span a range of responsiveness. For example, you might state that your target is to solve ninety percent of problems within four hours, and an additional nine percent within one business day. Stating such service targets is a way of communicating that situations will arise in which one business day is the best you can do, and that on rare occasions—in this case, no more than one percent—the situation will be completely new or unusually complex, and you'll need more time.

Exception Standards

Customers are entitled to expect that you will respond within your stated service level unless you specifically inform them otherwise. However, despite your best intention, situations will arise in which you can't meet that level because of intervening priorities or other unanticipated events. What is important is that customers are kept informed; those I've spoken to have expressed considerable frustration at not being told that their request will not be handled within the stated service-level period. These customers have all said they understand that sometimes their needs cannot be met as initially promised;

however, they object to not being informed when such situations arise.

To address this, a standard can be established that states that, in the event services cannot be delivered within the published period, the customer will be notified and given an estimate of when the service will be delivered. This is an exception standard that should be part of any set of service standards.

Incentives

In formulating service standards, consider how they can be used not only to inform customers of what they can reasonably expect, but also to create incentives for customers to take certain actions. For example, consider this service standard:

> *We will respond to ninety percent of calls within four hours of receipt of the call. We will give priority to customers whose departments have designated a PC coordinator as the first source of support within the customer department.*

The organization that established this standard wanted to encourage customers to participate in its new PC coordinator program, and as an incentive offered those who did so priority service. Of course, this particular incentive can work only when the number of participating departments is small; once many such departments have designated a coordinator, the standard would have to be revised. Nevertheless, it's an excellent example of how to phrase a service standard that, in one brief statement, communicates information about

- the service to be delivered

- the level of service responsiveness to be provided

- the method of setting service priorities

- the conditions customers must follow to obtain high-priority attention

- the consequences for customers who choose not to follow these conditions

Here is another example of a service standard that incorporates incentives:

We will provide immediate recovery assistance to customers who have lost data, provided that backups have been done in accordance with corporate guidelines. Otherwise, we will assist in recovery when staff resources become available.

For the support group that established this standard, immediate assistance meant as quickly as possible. Staff members concluded that they preferred to promise immediate assistance, and to do their best to respond expeditiously, rather than commit to a specific time frame. Like the preceding standard, this one also communicates the conditions of the service and describes how priorities will be set. It provides an incentive for customers to follow corporate guidelines for performing backups, but also allows customers the freedom to choose not to follow these guidelines by clarifying the consequences of such a decision. The expectations-managing value of this service standard is clear: This group will not abandon customers who violate standards, but neither should such customers expect that they will be given either immediate attention or top-priority attention.

Standards Based on Past Performance

Service standards provide a basis for communicating your service goals to customers. But nothing speaks on your behalf as well as evidence of past success. Announcing your commitment to solve ninety percent of problems within four hours may do little to create the expectations you want, if your performance for the previous six months falls far short of these service levels.

In fact, communicating such service levels may initially trigger skepticism until you are able to demonstrate your ability to respond at these levels. If, on the other hand, you resolved ninety-three percent of all problems within four hours during the previous six months, and ninety-seven percent within six hours, these statistics carry a great deal more credibility than promises of future performance. Customers may not find these service levels acceptable—they may need problems resolved within four hours ninety-eight percent of the time, rather than ninety-three percent—but this standard describes what they can realistically expect and provides a "that's not it" focal point for requesting improved responsiveness.

STANDARDS FOR SERVICES THAT GO AWRY

Situations often arise in which customers are eager to know what to expect, but for which you are reluctant to establish a service standard. For example, you might not want a formal standard that states: "Recovery from power outages: two hours," because such a standard might lead customers to fear that such outages are going to happen so often as to justify such a standard. Nevertheless, in circumstances that are an exception to normal functioning—and particularly those that are an unnerving exception to normal functioning—the uncertainty of the situation makes many customers want not only to be advised about the status of the situation, but to be updated regularly. How well you do that can strongly influence customer satisfaction.

I discovered firsthand the value of status reports the time I was stuck on a chair lift. Initially, I was relieved when the attendants removed my uncertainty by telling us it would take an hour to get the lift moving again. At least I knew what to expect. Unfortunately, the repair took more than an hour: one hour and twelve minutes, to be exact. And those final twelve minutes felt as long as the hour that preceded them, because once the one-hour mark passed, I no longer knew what to expect. No one told us whether rescue was imminent or still hours away. I was not a happy skier.

Regular Updates

What kind of service standard will help keep customers calm in uncertain conditions in which even *you* don't know what to expect? One effective way to do this was aptly demonstrated when I was sitting on a plane that was still parked at the gate long after the scheduled departure time. This airline was unusual. First, a crew member told us there was a delay. Since we hadn't budged an inch, that much was obvious. Then he admitted that the plane had a mechanical problem and the crew had no idea how long the delay would last. As annoying as the delay was, I admired the airline for being willing to acknowledge this situation. The crew member then said he'd keep us informed by reporting the status every fifteen minutes. That impressed me, but what impressed me most was this: He told us he'd report the status every fifteen minutes, *even if he had nothing new to tell us.*

This is an excellent example of a service standard for dealing with the customer's need to know what's happening. The airline personnel did four things that are critical in managing expectations in a time of uncertainty.

- They kept us informed about the status of the delay. They didn't just leave us wondering and fuming.

- They kept us informed on a specific schedule—and the speed with which they announced that schedule suggested that it was part of a previously established service standard.

- They kept us informed even when it was just to tell us they had nothing new to report. If they had chosen to update us only when they had something new to tell us, we might have quickly begun to wonder whether they had nothing new to report or had simply forgotten to tell us.

- They told us their plan to keep us informed, so that we knew precisely what to expect. They could have simply given us an update every fifteen minutes without telling us they intended to do so, but that might not have prevented us from wondering between updates when the next one would take place. By stating their intent to keep us informed, they did the most important thing of all: *They managed our expectations about how they would manage our expectations.*

The existence of this service standard not only reduced passenger uncertainty, but also avoided a situation of uncertainty among airline personnel about what they should tell us and when. Your customers may appreciate a similar level of responsiveness from you when problems arise. Therefore, identify those situations that create the greatest uncertainty for your customers and establish a service standard that will enable you to keep them informed about the status of the situation. The result will be a reduced level of agitation both for your customers and for you.

Acknowledgment of Error

When you are stuck in a chair lift high above the ground or sitting in a plane delayed at the gate, you don't have to wonder if something is amiss; it's obvious. In some situations, though, problems occur that customers don't know about, yet would appreciate being advised of so they can plan accordingly. As Frederick Brooks reminds us, bad news, late and without warning, is unsettling to customers.[1] Therefore, even if a formal service standard doesn't exist for such situations, an ad hoc decision should be made to keep customers informed. That was the view of a fellow who took a day off to stay home and await delivery of his living room furniture. When the appointed time came and went, he called the company, and found out he wasn't even on the roster for the day!

But this is not just another they-didn't-show-up-and-they-didn't-call story. It seems the company had discontinued the furniture he had ordered, and had never bothered to tell him. If he hadn't called them, he'd still be sitting there—probably on the floor—waiting. (The story has a happy ending. To make amends, the company gave him a substantial discount on its new line of furniture, thereby turning an angry customer into a happier one. Taking action to turn a negative situation into a positive one is also part of managing expectations.)

In working with customers, simply ask yourself regularly, Is there anyone I ought to update on the status of efforts that will affect them? Are any of my customers sitting at the other end of the phone line, mumbling and grumbling and wondering when (or whether) I'll contact them? Is anyone waiting for work I'm doing who might feel better with an update?

SOLUTIONS GUARANTEED (OR PROBLEMS RETURNED)

Don't expect the impossible from service standards. Even the best standards won't cause truly unreasonable customers to act reasonably. However, the very existence of service standards can contribute to improved delivery of your services and better relationships with customers, because all parties involved have a clearer understanding of what to expect of each other. And they provide a focal point for negotiation and discussion about what customers need as circumstances change.

Therefore, think about which category of setting service standards, or variation of this category, best fits your own situation. Then establish service standards and develop a plan for implementing them. And if you already have service standards in place, periodically review them for their relevance to current services and for their adequacy in meeting present and future needs. After all, standards for changing typewriter ribbons may not be quite as relevant as they used to be.

NOTES

[1]Frederick P. Brooks, Jr., *The Mythical Man-Month* (Reading, Mass.: Addison-Wesley Publishing Co., 1975), p. 20.

11

When Appropriate, Just Say Whoa

How to say no so it sounds like yes

A PC specialist was heading down the hall to help a customer in distress when he was sidetracked by another customer who had a problem. Off he went to help the second customer. "How could I say no?" he asked when we discussed this situation. "The person needed my help, and I wanted to be responsive." Responsive? The first customer didn't think he was.

When customers ask for help, do you find it hard to say no, even when you can justifiably do so? If so, read on, because this guideline is about the art and science of saying no: the *art* of saying no when you must and the *science* of establishing policies and practices to reduce the number of circumstances in which saying no is necessary.

SAYING YES AND SAYING NO

Saying no may seem to conflict with the very notion of customer service, but it doesn't, provided it's done at appropriate times and in appropriate ways. That's why this guideline, unlike all the others in this book, is prefaced by "when appropriate." You have to make a choice: If you want to provide consistently high-quality service, you can't do everything for everyone. And if you insist on doing everything for everyone, you will not be able to provide consistently high-quality service. Contradictory though it might seem at first, those most driven to be responsive may at times be the biggest contributors to poor customer service.

The Connection Between Actions and Expectations

You simply can't do it all; if you think you can, you're deluding yourself. But you're not deluding customers to whom you make commitments you can't keep. After all, it's not making commitments that counts; it's delivering on those commitments. There is an intimate connection between your actions and the expectations these actions create: Every time you respond to a request, you reinforce the customer for making that request. Every time you provide nanosecond-level responsiveness, you lead customers to expect the same the next time around, whether or not they need this speed of response. And every time you rescue customers from situations caused by a violation of standards, you lead them to expect you to take responsibility for their irresponsibility.

In doing all these things, you tell the customer, as clearly as if you used words, that it's all right to do the same again tomorrow . . . and next week . . . and next month. Yet, it's precisely because of the connection between actions and expectations that the reverse is also true: If you take longer or do less or defer action—when appropriate—that's what customers will come to expect. Sometimes, deliberately doing just a little bit less is the best thing you can do for yourself. And sometimes, being just a little less available is the best way to reduce dependence on you and to promote customer self-sufficiency.

The Limits of Service Orientation

When I ask people why they feel they have to be so responsive, they usually tell me, "We're a service organization, so we have to be service-oriented." I've heard this response from every organizational level from front-line customer service staff to upper-level management. It's difficult to fault anyone for being service-oriented, but even a service orientation has limits that are obvious as soon as you think about them. For example,

- If your workload doubled, would you remain equally responsive to all customers?

- If a customer asked you to develop a system that would solve Trivial Problem A, but would create Much Bigger Problem B, would you automatically accept the request?

- If you were asked to give up all vacations and weekends for the next two years in order to better serve customers, would you do it?

Clearly, even if you're service-oriented, circumstances exist in which you might reject the request, redirect it, reassign it, reconsider it, defer it, or at least question its appropriateness. ("I can't do brain surgery, but let me refer you to someone else who can. . . .") So why not take these actions more often?

The Path of Least Resistance

For many people, doing what customers ask is simply the path of least resistance. Despite growing workloads and declining energy levels, it's often easier to respond to the request, even if grudgingly, than to face the potentially negative consequences of saying no—even if there is no evidence that such consequences have occurred in the past or are likely to in the future. That's why policies and practices that support saying no, when appropriate, make sense.

A variety of factors cause people to have difficulty saying no to customer requests. Some have difficulty because they want to avoid being criticized for unresponsiveness. Some don't want to offend or disappoint customers. Some fear being chewed out by management or chewed up by demanding customers. Some view their efforts as a way to silence squeaky wheels, even if only temporarily. For some, it is a fear of being disliked.

However, there are those like Mike, my former IS director, who have no trouble saying no. I once sent him a proposal which he rejected. I changed a few points, and resubmitted it. Another rejection. Thinking he might change his mind over time, I waited awhile, then tried once again. This time he returned it with a little "From the desk of . . ." sheet clipped to it, on which he had stamped:

Absolutely
Positively
NO!

I got the message.

Mike succeeded in using humor to get his point across. Think about ways you can do the same, and in the process, reduce the tension sometimes inherent in rejecting a request for assistance.

SAYING WHOA

Fortunately, saying no is not the only option you have in

responding to customers to whom it would be best not to say yes. In some situations, it is both acceptable and appropriate to say *whoa* to customer requests. It isn't saying no, but at the same time it isn't quite saying yes. Consider these ways of saying whoa:

- "I would like to give you my undivided attention, but I'm busy now. Let's plan a convenient time tomorrow to talk about this."

- "I'll help you this time, so you'll know how to handle this type of problem yourself, but it really is your responsibility. I need to be sure you understand that if it happens again, we may not have anyone available to help you."

- "I'd help if I could, but my workload for the next three months is already bigger than I can handle."

- "We must give customers who use company-standard products highest priority. Since this isn't one of those products, we'll get to you as soon as we can, but I'm afraid it may be a few days."

These responses illustrate that you often have options concerning how you respond, such as deferring action, explaining why you can't provide the requested assistance, or suggesting ways in which customers can help themselves. Obviously, you have to use good judgment in deciding when and whether to use such responses. Each is appropriate at certain times and inappropriate or politically unwise at other times, and all may require a change in wording to feel more natural to you.

Benefits

Consider what saying whoa—in just a few words—accomplishes for you:

- It buys time to do many things, such as completing one task before starting another, thinking about the best way to help a customer, adjusting your priorities, and even taking a long-overdue five-minute break.

- It emphasizes that you are service-oriented, but that you nevertheless must make choices in whom you can help.

- It signals your intention to abide by standards, and tells customers not to expect you to help them when they choose to do otherwise.

- It communicates that customers also have responsibilities, and clarifies what these responsibilities are.

- It creates incentives for customers to consider alternative sources of support.

- It promotes self-sufficiency, because customers forced to wait sometimes find ways to solve their problems themselves.

- Most important, it helps you create expectations that more closely match what you can reasonably and realistically deliver.

If situations already exist in which you can benefit from saying whoa, why wait until the unthinkable forces you to do so? Why not address those situations now, while the choice is yours? In fact, several of the previous guidelines, such as those on avoiding conflicting messages, clarifying perceptions, and setting service standards, can be viewed as formal ways of saying whoa. By acting on these guidelines, you give your customers a clearer idea of what they can expect of you and what you expect of them; the result is that you work more effectively together and have fewer situations in which verbal whoas are needed. But there is still more you can do.

The Hit-by-a-Bus Test

The best way to begin doing more is by taking the Hit-by-a-Bus test. This is a "test" for you and your coworkers to take to simulate a situation in which it's easy to say whoa:

THE HIT-BY-A-BUS TEST

Imagine that your department is seriously overworked and understaffed. You can't possibly handle an additional thing.

Suddenly, a key member of your department goes berserk, races from the building, and is hit by a proverbial bus.

As everyone knows, it takes a long time to recover from injuries caused by proverbial buses. Given this, what changes would you make to manage your department's workload and still provide quality services?

This test concludes when you have come up with answers that satisfy you. You are the sole judge of whether you have passed.

Whether it's a proverbial bus that comes veering around the corner, out of control, or a not-so-proverbial change in staffing or workload, the time to think about how you can improve your situation is now, while it's under your control. Spend some time as a group brainstorming about what you'd like to do differently. Develop a specific program of improvements, and begin immediately to act on it.

PUTTING WHOA INTO PRACTICE

The following ideas provide a focal point for thinking about ways to help you say whoa through policies and practices:

Review Your Department's Request Process

Your service request process should function so that customers know what to expect of you at the time they solicit your help, and so that you are able to identify those situations in which you can justifiably say whoa. For example,

• **Provide a single collection point for all service requests submitted to your department, so that you can identify similar or related requests.** Customers, even within the same department, often don't know of each other's requests. Similarly, work groups, even within a given service department, often don't know when they are handling overlapping, related, or redundant customer requests. Make it as easy for yourself as you can to gain an overall perspective of the requests you receive.

• **Advise customers about their responsibilities in working with you.** For example, if you typically require customers to specify constraints, estimate benefits, justify their need, or document criteria for success—or you would like them to do such things—make sure they are aware of these requirements from the outset. Don't rely strictly on verbal communications of such information. Even if you have already documented these measures elsewhere, summarize them on your request form to ensure your customers are aware of them.

• **Create a formal rejection process to make it easier to communicate your reasons for not accepting a particular request.** By creating a menu of typical reasons for rejecting or deferring requests, you can standardize the rejection process, and at the same time increase customers' understanding of what they must do to have their requests accepted and acted upon. If it is your policy always to reject requests that fall short of certain criteria, such as providing cost savings of less than a specified dollar limit, identify these criteria as part of your request process.

• **Educate customers to know the issues they should consider, alternatives they should evaluate, and information they should obtain before requesting your assistance, so that you can address their needs expediently.** Customers are more likely to do some advance footwork if they understand what you want them to do and why. For example, by educating them in some of the information-gathering and problem-solving issues described in this book, you will be helping them to improve the quality of the requests they submit.

• **Ensure that adequate communication exists in your department so that everyone knows what projects are in progress.** A total duplication of effort is rare, but failure to take advantage of the synergies among the efforts of multiple staff members is common. If staff members are geographically dispersed, communication among those who perform similar functions is difficult, yet extremely important if redundancies are to be minimized. Develop a tracking system so that you know when several of you have been contacted by the same customer or are engaged in similar efforts.

• **Clarify your priority-setting policy.** If objective criteria exist by which requests are ordered into a priority sequence, use your request process to inform customers of these criteria. Doing so reduces the need to turn away customers, or to respond to endless requests for an explanation when their request does not make it into the top ten.

Establish Whoa-Based Service Standards

As described in Chapter 10, service standards help you clarify customers' expectations about your services. Equally important, they can help you manage your expectations of yourself, by formally giving you permission to say whoa—and maybe even requiring you to do so. For example, a service standard that restricts support to a specified product portfolio can be helpful to staff members who might be tempted to bypass standards when confronted by particularly persuasive customers. In addition, service standards can be used to establish internal targets so that employees can manage their expectations of themselves.

Service standards can also be established for classifying problems or requests according to urgency. For example, in an Urgent-High-Medium-Low classification, the Urgent designation might signify the need for immediate attention, High within four hours, Medium within a day, and so on—or whatever classification system best fits your services. This type of classification system allows customers to manage their expectations of you: When they describe problems as, say, Medium priority, they are acknowledging they will wait the specified time period for a resolution.

Contrary to prevalent fears that customers will declare all requests Urgent if given the opportunity, the experiences of several organizations suggest this is usually not the case, provided that customers trust their response will be handled within the allotted time period. Be sure, however, that you have a common understanding of the terms you use to classify urgency. While writing this chapter, I received a call from a woman who asked me to send her a package of material. She said she'd like it quickly. Fine, I said, knowing that my local expectations-managing delivery service could get it to her the next morning. "Yes," she continued, "I'd like to see it within the next month." I thanked her for clarifying that point, and posted a note on my bulletin board reminding me to stop making assumptions.

Identify Alternative Resources

If you are frequently called upon for work that is more appropriately handled elsewhere, an awareness of alternative resources can help you say whoa. A list of alternative resources might include other departments, other staff within your own department, external services, classes, documentation, vendor support lines, online help, or customers who possess specialized technical expertise.

Identify the most common situations in which you can justifiably either divert work to these alternative resources, or call upon them to help. Ensure a consensus within your own group so you can present a consistent list of recommendations to customers. But don't keep this list a secret; communicate it to customers so they, too, know the options available to them. The more familiar they are with the full range of options, the more likely they are to seek support from these alternatives rather than remain dependent on you.

These alternative sources of support can be incorporated into your whoa-based service standard. For example, customers may be told they should first try to solve their problem using online sources of support. If that doesn't resolve their problem, they should seek assistance from someone in their own department. Next, if necessary, they should contact customer coordinators assigned to provide local support. Their final option, after trying all of these, is to contact the technical support department.

In addition to promoting customer self-sufficiency and directing customers to the nearest sources of support, this type of support strategy also lets customers know what you expect them to do before contacting you. By publishing these alternative sources of support and the sequence in which customers should use them, you can ask customers who contact you if they have taken these required steps; if they haven't, you have an objective basis for saying whoa.

Say Whoa to Your Manager (When Appropriate, of Course)

For some groups, the problem isn't overly demanding customers as much as a manager who expects more than is reasonable. If you face this type of situation, consider whether you might be at least partially responsible for it. Perhaps your situation is like that of the participant in one of my seminars who complained that his manager was relentlessly upbeat and happy-go-lucky, all the while giving his staff more and more work. The manager loved to come to work; the staff, however, didn't. "What do you do when your manager gives all of you this excessive amount of work?" I asked him. His response: "What can we do? He's the boss, so we do it."

"Have you ever told him that you find it difficult to handle all this work?" I asked.

"Well . . . no."

By limiting their reaction to private mumblings and grum-blings, these individuals prevented their manager from realiz-ing that anything problematic was taking place. By accepting the work, they were meeting his expectation that they could handle it. Worse, they were reinforcing him for piling it on. It's no wonder he always smiled. Who wouldn't, in his situation?

If your manager expects too much of you, your best strate-gy may be to confront the situation. One department manager did just this when she was put in charge of two additional departments "just temporarily," she was told, until replace-ments could be found. Her workload became unbearable. After several months of "just a little longer," she decided she'd had enough. She wrote a letter to her vice president and quit. No, she didn't resign from the company; she quit one of the three jobs. Her "resignation" was immediately accepted, and some-one else was appointed to fill the position. Had she done noth-ing, she might still be hearing promises of "any day now," while continuing to hold three jobs.[1] (Unfortunately, she failed to anticipate the downside. Once she was in charge of only two departments, management felt she must now have substantial free time, and assigned her some hefty projects she'd been spared previously. To paraphrase a familiar saying, be careful what you wish for in managing expectations; you just might get it.)

Interestingly, several managers have told me they've urged their staff to say no to customers more often. These managers want their staff to be more selective about how they allocate their time, so they can provide the maximum possible impact with their limited resources. Some of these managers claim, however, that despite urging their staff to do less, staff members continue to work at and beyond peak levels. Further discussion often reveals, however, that although they urge their staff to say no, they do so only in very vague terms. They don't establish internal standards so that staff will know precisely when they can and cannot say no. In the absence of clear guidelines, staff members simply continue at their accustomed levels.

Although the risk of saying whoa is that it will trigger complaints about unresponsiveness, such complaints are not necessarily bad. As the group described in Chapter 9 discovered, the absence of complaints can be dangerous: You may not know what your customers are thinking, even as they take their business elsewhere. It's for this reason that some astute managers view complaints as having positive value. According to one IS director, whose view provides considerable food for thought, "If no one is complaining, it could mean we're doing too much. I would prefer to back off a little at a time until customers complain. Then we can distinguish between just right and too much." His notion of an absence of complaints as an indicator of excessive customer service is worth thinking about. You may have more leeway to say whoa than you realize.

Specify Who Has Authority to Accept Customer Requests

In certain environments, such as help desk support, all staff members may be authorized to respond to all calls. In other environments, such as systems development, the authority to accept a request or respond to a problem may need to be precisely defined so that staff members clearly understand both the scope and the limits of their authority.

I realized the need for such clarification from Jim, a senior analyst on my IS staff who was Mr. Customer Service Personified: If he saw a task that needed attention, he tackled it. At one point, I was in the midst of sensitive negotiations with the manager of an unreasonably demanding customer department, and I had informed the manager I was putting all requests from her department on hold until we negotiated some ground rules.

One day, the manager mentioned a service request her department had recently submitted to us. I responded in my I'm-in-charge-here voice, "You know we're not working on your service requests at the moment." She said, "What do you mean you're not working on it? It's already done."

Sure enough, Jim had found the service request in our request queue, and without getting his project leader's approval or telling anyone he was working on it, he undertook and completed the project. His rationale was that the customer needed the work done, so he did it.

In so doing, Jim undermined my negotiating position. I was sure I could hear the manager suppress a hearty laugh at the other end of the phone when she told me the project was already completed. Jim's service orientation was commendable, but it was clear my department needed improved internal communication as well as clarification of its procedures.

Identify Services and Activities That Can Be Cut

Many service groups devote too much effort to activities that are either nonessential or that deliver too little payoff. In the process, they become diverted from responding to customer requests that are perfectly reasonable, but that begin to appear unreasonable simply because they are part of an ever-growing workload.

To address this issue, consider whether all the services you deliver are worthwhile. Ask customers to identify what services have lower priority. Consider whether a different division of responsibilities between your group and other systems groups or customers would enable you to provide better service.

If you examine how you spend your time, you may find that a large percentage of the important results you generate come from a small percentage of your effort, and conversely a large percentage of your effort is generating minimal or insignificant results. Identify efforts that yield the least payback, especially relative to the time invested, and cut or reduce them. If you support multiple customer departments, identify the customers on whom you spend the bulk of your time, and analyze how you can support their needs more effectively.

It's also a worthwhile exercise to measure your unproductive time. This is time spent on unproductive efforts—you can define this any way you want. For example, it could be work that members of your group wouldn't need to do if others, such as customers, managers, or vendors, sufficiently fulfilled their responsibilities. You may spend unproductive time on work that is repetitive and labor-intensive, and that keeps you from responding to requests you might otherwise view as reasonable.

Establish a definition of unproductive time; then track the time your group spends on these unproductive efforts for a period of a month or two, and put a dollar value on it. If that value is high—and some managers have found that it adds up to tens of thousands of dollars over the course of a year—you have concrete evidence of a serious problem in the way you are delivering your services or in the cooperation you're getting from others.[2] This evidence can provide the clout necessary to make some long overdue changes.

An important way to reduce unproductive time is to eliminate redundant efforts. Technical support staff are particularly prone to this situation, especially when they respond to similar questions repeatedly, yet do little to identify ways to prevent such questions from arising in the first place. I think of this problem as one of eliminating repeat business. If the time spent on redundant activities keeps you from tackling higher-payoff efforts, analyze the sources and causes of this "repeat business," and identify ways to eliminate it.

Develop Scripts That Can Help You Just Say Whoa

For many people, it's not the idea of saying whoa that's hard; it's finding the right words to use. If this is your problem, collaborate with your coworkers to develop scripts you can use when it's appropriate to say whoa. Here are a few to add to those previously listed:

- "I'm right in the middle of something. Can I get back to you in an hour?"

- "I can't help you, but let me transfer you to someone who can."

- "I can help you faster if you'll get me the following information."

- "Will it cause you a problem if we put this on hold until next week?"

SEEKING NO HELP

Sometimes, of course, you really do need to say no. In that case, you want to be sure it sounds clearly like no, not whoa. For this, too, scripts can help. Create your own scripts by observing the techniques of those who are good at it, such as Mike and his "Absolutely Positively NO!"

Solicit the assistance of those who can help you. I once had a project leader working for me who had both a strong service orientation and the ability to say no with ease. When I knew I had to refuse a request, but felt my resolve weakening, I would ask him to help me. It was a fine arrangement—except when he said no to my own assignments. He'd look down at me from on high and say "NO, I won't!"

But I'd just look up at him, smile, and say "YES, you will!" And he did.

Rank has its benefits.

NOTES

[1]Stephen Covey describes a similar experience he had when he was a director of university relations and asked a staff writer to handle some urgent tasks for him. The writer produced a list of more than two dozen projects he was already working on, along with performance criteria and due dates. He then asked Covey, "Which of these projects would you like me to delay or cancel to satisfy your request?" This led Covey to conclude that these new requests were not that important, after all. Stephen R. Covey, *The 7 Habits of Highly Effective People* (New York: Simon & Schuster, 1989), p. 157.

[2]Frederick Brooks describes the findings of a manager who tracked time usage after determining that jobs were consistently taking twice as long as estimated. According to Brooks, "machine downtime, higher-priority short unrelated jobs, meetings, paperwork, company business, sickness, personal time, etc." accounted for the discrepancy. "In short, the estimates made unrealistic assumptions about the number of technical work hours per man-year." Frederick P. Brooks, Jr., *The Mythical Man-Month* (Reading, Mass.: Addison-Wesley Publishing Co., 1975), pp. 89-90.

12

Build Win-Win Relationships
Win friends and influence customers

When I finally ski-tested the blue jacket I told you about in Chapter 8, I discovered that it was not quite perfect, and took it to my tailor for alterations. He said it would be ready in a week. When I went to pick it up, it wasn't ready. I was annoyed. This wasn't customer service; it was customer *dis*service. He could have called me and saved me the trip. I thought about switching tailors.

That's how I would have reacted if this tailor had been a stranger, but he wasn't. I'm a long-time customer. We chat and exchange pleasantries. He does good work and has given me rush service on several occasions. This one time, when he slipped, I was able to shrug it off. "No problem," I told him, "I'll be back next week."

Of all the ideas in this book, none, in my view, can contribute as powerfully to your ability to successfully manage expectations as building and maintaining relationships. This guideline appears as the last of the twelve to emphasize that when you get along well with your customers, it becomes easier to carry out all the other ideas in this book. It also becomes easier to identify and discuss your expectations of each other, thereby improving the odds of success in achieving your shared goals.

The fortunate thing about relationships is that they can evolve naturally; every time you meet with customers, you are strengthening your relationship with them. But you can do numerous things to accelerate the process, as this guideline describes.

CUSTOMERS AS ALLIES

In recent years, "partnership" has become a popular buzzword to describe a relationship with customers that contrasts sharply with the less cooperative relationships of the past. Not everyone is pleased with the notion of a partnership. Some service providers resist the idea and maintain a firm grip on their us/them attitude. Others claim to support the idea, but view it to mean "Let's you and I agree to do things my way." Most, happily, recognize that win-win relationships are more likely to lead to successful outcomes.

Customer Contact

Unfortunately, building relationships with customers is not a snap-of-the-fingers process. To start, you have to view every contact with a customer as an opportunity for relationship building. And "every contact" must mean more than a quick hello while running the other way. You have to spend time meeting, talking, and getting to know each other. You have to develop trust in each other, and a mutual belief that you'll each do what's reasonable so that you both achieve your goals.

Meeting, talking, and building trust are not activities you add to your to-do list, and then cross off once you've done them. They must stay on your list forever. Developing a bond with customers takes work, and once you've succeeded in creating that bond, you have to continually work at maintaining it; otherwise, it breaks down or simply dissipates.

Many of the groups to whom I've provided relationship-building assistance concede that they haven't done enough to build new relationships or improve existing ones. Most say they want to do more. The members of one such department went a step further. They concluded that they would like to do more to improve relationships, not just with existing and prospective customers, but also with those who had no immediate need for their department's services. Their reasoning was that, given all the reorganizations the company was experiencing, the non-customers of today could easily become the prime customers of tomorrow, and it would be worthwhile to spend some time paving the way for future win-win relationships.

The fact that this department was part of an IS organization that charged for its services made this decision a sound one. A competitor's services may be cheaper or demonstrably better, but people often buy from their friends simply because they're friends. Even if you don't charge for your services, building relationships with future customers makes sense. The hardest time to build relationships is when you're in the midst of responding to immediate demands; by starting now to develop relationships throughout your organization, you'll be ahead of the game.

Reputation for Performance

Of course, it helps in building relationships if you have a positive reputation for meeting customer needs. If customers perceive that you've met their expectations before, they're more likely to see you as someone who will do so next time around.

People tend to expect a repeat of what they've experienced before. And that's why it's so difficult to develop a positive relationship if you've acquired a negative reputation.

Therefore, if you already have a positive reputation, recognize its value in relationship building. On the other hand, if your past efforts have earned you a less than positive reputation, you have some work to do to gain your customers' trust and respect. And if you're working with customers who distrust you because of their negative experiences with others, you may need to focus explicit attention on improving that relationship and earning their trust and confidence.

TECHNIQUES FOR RELATIONSHIP BUILDING

Relationship-building techniques range from those that are formal, scheduled, and carefully planned to those that are casual and ad hoc. Here are some proven techniques to consider.

Arrange Department-Specific Meetings

One of the simplest approaches to relationship building is to periodically hold a brief, informal meeting with each customer department. Such meetings may not be necessary when you work exclusively with one customer whom you come to know well, but they can be especially effective when you work with multiple departments and have little in-depth time to devote to any one of them. Even one such meeting a year with each department will strengthen your relationship with that department.

Unlike the checkpoint assessments described in Chapter 9, these meetings are strictly for the purpose of getting to know each other better, and should therefore avoid issues pertaining to current projects or services. The agenda can revolve around a discussion both of their priorities and concerns and of your own. The customer-focused questions listed in Chapter 7 make ideal conversation-starters for this type of meeting.

Some systems groups plan a meeting every month or two with a different customer department. Although they discuss the department's goals, priorities, and concerns, they manage expectations from the outset by emphasizing that the purpose of the meeting is to broaden their understanding of each other, and that customers should not necessarily expect action to be taken on the issues they discuss. In fact, these meetings are a perfect place to raise the issue of expectations, and to stress that you'd like to ensure that your expectations and theirs are in sync.

Aside from strengthening relationships, these meetings have other benefits: They can help you reassess your own services on a continuing basis and determine what changes, if any, you may need to plan. They provide an ongoing means of assessing customer satisfaction, and can supplement or even replace surveys. They also help in improving your understanding of the business in general, as well as your customers' specific subset of the business—and at the same time, help your customers improve their understanding of your business.

How often you hold these meetings is not as important as that you hold them systematically. They are too easy to postpone, just "until things slow down a little," as several managers have stated, while explaining that they mean to spend more time with their customers, but just haven't gotten to it yet. Those who make it an ongoing responsibility claim that it's well worth their time. And most customers asked to spend an hour or two in such meetings are willing and even eager to do so. In fact, several such customers have commented that it's rare for anyone from IS to ask about them, and they're pleased to have the opportunity to talk about their work. The outcome of this exchange is the growth of a sense of camaraderie that fosters a much closer working relationship thereafter.

Conduct Cross-Functional Exchanges

If you meet with one customer department every month or two, and you support as many departments as I did when I was a manager of end-user computing, it could take several revolutions of Mars before you meet with all of them. In that situation, a cross-functional exchange can be an excellent way to meet with representatives of several customer departments at one time.

This type of exchange can take numerous forms; one I particularly like is a meeting to exchange views on a preselected subject. While sports scores or commuter woes might ably serve as the selected subject, topics that revolve around the impact of technology on customers can be eye-openers because systems staff often underestimate that impact. I've found that such meetings work best when the formal agenda serves simply as a guide. The exchange of ideas that takes place as hot buttons emerge is of much greater relationship-building value than reaching the next item on an agenda.

One of the most valuable benefits of such exchanges is that they reveal differences in viewpoint that had never been openly discussed before. In one meeting I facilitated for ten systems staff and ten customer representatives, systems participants were surprised by the intensity of their customers' frustration with the complexity and duration of the PC acquisition process. The systems staff had not previously realized that their customers viewed them as responsible for this cumbersome process, especially since they always completed their acquisition tasks expeditiously, and were themselves frustrated by the subsequent delays that routinely occurred. As the discussion proceeded, numerous flaws in the process surfaced. Then and there, with no one driving them to do it, several IS and customer participants volunteered to collaborate and improve the acquisition process. Such fruitful outcomes can't be guaranteed, but they take place with surprising frequency, and they pave the way for major boosts in interdepartmental cooperation thereafter.

Cross-functional exchanges also improve communication among diverse customer areas. It's not unusual to hear representatives from different business departments comment that they never really understood each other's perspectives before. An improved understanding among customers may not be an explicit objective of a cross-functional exchange, but when it happens, the departments involved become better able to manage their expectations of each other. That, needless to say, can simplify your job enormously when it entails managing expectations across departmental boundaries.

Systems managers sometimes assume that customers lack the time or inclination to participate in meetings of this kind, but my experience has been just the reverse. When customers are personally invited, they typically accept with enthusiasm and participate actively. I recall one business manager who told systems participants at the end of a half-day exchange, "You know, we ought to meet like this more often." That is the mark of a successful exchange.

Accept Responsibility for Your Mistakes

When you make a mistake that affects others, acknowledge it and do something to set it right. People are so used to seeing others pass the buck that you can take them by surprise if you admit to your mistakes, especially if you do so publicly. Admitting to small mistakes can build credibility with customers; interestingly, bigger mistakes sometimes seem not so big to them later. Simply acknowledging your mistakes can build trust and strengthen your relationship far beyond what you might anticipate from the impact of the incident itself.

For example, one of my IS departments supported a department whose manager viewed the IS division as a bottomless pit of excuses for why work wasn't done on time. (A rather accurate view, I have to admit.) Early in my relationship with her, she had been authorized to use a specified number of mainframe cycles in database queries on a certain project. I had promised her a monthly report with which she could track her department's usage, but due to problems at my end I was unable to deliver these reports the first two months.

When the reports were finally run, I sent them to her with a note explaining that the delay was our fault. I told her that she shouldn't be held accountable for statistics we hadn't been able to provide, and that I wasn't going to charge her account for the two months of usage. She was amazed. No one in IS had ever admitted to being at fault, she told me months later, after our relationship had become a mutually supportive one.

This technique of taking responsibility obviously won't work if you err too often or too seriously, but it's almost worth making a mistake just to have a reason to apologize. Almost.

Remember the Basic Courtesies

The basic courtesies are things you already know: Advise customers of upcoming changes. Give them a chance to have their say—and when they do, listen. Return phone calls. Acknowledge the validity of their views even if you don't agree. Send thank-you notes. It's often gestures such as these that make the difference in whether customers work with you or against you.

My staff discovered the impact of basic courtesies on relationship building, thanks to one particular customer. Colleen was a source of constant frustration, because she always insisted that she was right and everyone else was wrong. She would regularly bombard us with, "You know, you really ought to . . ." Not a thing we did ever met her expectations.

One day, probably in a fit of desperation, one of my project teams decided to try a basic courtesies experiment with Colleen. Without offering her any explanation, they started asking her to elaborate on her ideas. They began to listen to her more carefully, even when they didn't agree with her. They acknowledged her perspective. They talked with her and showered her with attention. In the process—and no one was more amazed than they were—they did more than gain her respect; they actually became friends with her. I knew something strange was going on when Colleen started showing up regularly to spend coffee breaks with my staff. What a metamorphosis! She'd become one of us.

The result of this experiment was that Colleen, like the customer acceptance testing team I described in Chapter 9, became one of our greatest supporters. Like them, she not only came to see our perspective; she became our mouthpiece to her own management, thereby enhancing our credibility with her superiors. And we, in turn, began not only to consider her perspective, but to welcome it, because it helped us do a better job for our customers.

Confront Negative Relationships

It's not the place of this book to recommend that you experiment on your customers, but taking steps to turn negative relationships into positive ones can certainly create a better climate for discussing your expectations of each other. By contrast to the subtle and time-consuming approach my staff used with Colleen, direct discussion can be a quicker and surprisingly effective way to improve a problem relationship. Pam, a software specialist, tried the direct approach with a high-level customer manager whom she and her coworkers described as impatient, pushy, and verbally abusive.

One day, the manager barged into the software group's area, interrupted their weekly meeting, and in front of Pam's peers, loudly scolded her for some perceived misdeed. Pam was so diminutive and soft-spoken that it was difficult to believe anyone would treat her this way, but according to her coworkers, such behavior was the norm for this manager. Yet, all of them, viewing the manager as being at too high a level to risk offending, had refrained from taking any action.

The next day, Pam went to the manager and explained that being treated that way was humiliating, and that she would prefer it not happen again. She said that if there was a problem, she'd address it, but that a public attack was not the means to that end. This was no master strategy; she simply expressed how she felt—and it worked beyond Pam's expectations: The manager not only began to treat Pam with respect, but also became more reasonable and less aggressive with the entire department.

Was this turnaround a one-of-a-kind experience? Not at all. In many similar situations that have since been reported to me, the customer not only apologizes, but becomes a source of support. In some cases, the turnaround is almost startling.[1] In fact, the simple act of confronting people about their behavior not only eliminates the problem, but changes the relationship from negative to positive.

Why do people act in these contrary ways in the first place? Maybe it's their way of getting attention. They may be people for whom the wrath of others is better than being ignored. Sometimes, people act this way simply because no one has told them to stop. That's what makes squeaky wheels so effective. Sometimes, people are driven by deep-rooted causes you can't hope to unearth. Sometimes, they just don't know any better, or they're mimicking someone else who doesn't know any better. In all cases, the failure to request that these people discontinue this behavior reinforces their expectation that it will be tolerated. Yet simply saying, "I don't like it. Please stop!" is sometimes all it takes not only to stop the problem, but to dramatically improve the relationship.

Be careful, though, with your attempts to reverse negative relationships. In discussing how to improve their relationship with a particular customer, members of one customer support group suggested taking a personal approach. Their idea was to find ways to compliment the customer and to comment on such things as photos of family members or other mementos in the customer's office. The group liked this idea, but I urged caution. A little such attention may help; a lot can backfire. I envisioned all twelve members of the group, one by one, wandering into the customer's office the following week, gushing, "Oh, what beautiful grandchildren you have!" Whatever approaches you select to relationship building, be sure to use them in moderation, and consider how these attempts might fail before you proceed.

Don't Take It Personally

My most pronounced insight regarding a negative relationship came from Charlie, the division manager who was my most difficult customer back when I was an IS manager. Although I worked with Charlie's division for what seemed like life plus ninety-nine years, my relationship with him never became a positive one. We completed the system we had developed, implemented it, and enjoyed seeing it successfully meet our customers' needs. During this entire period, Charlie never once acknowledged our efforts. As we moved into the next phase, a manager in Charlie's division gradually became my point of contact. Some time later, she told me that Charlie had been transferred to another division.

I didn't see Charlie for a couple of months after that. Then one day, I saw him in the hall. Having never let him in on how much I disliked him, I approached him as upbeat as ever, and told him I heard he'd been transferred. I'll never forget his response.

"Yes," he said, "and I'm so glad to be out of that department. There was so much pressure . . . so many deadlines . . . so much stress . . . so many demands . . . so much politics." He seemed much more relaxed. "At last," he said, "I feel as if I have some control over my existence." He actually smiled, and it struck me how rarely I had ever seen him smile. I couldn't believe the transformation. Gone was the hostile person I had worked with, and in its place was one of the gentlest people I had ever met. For the first time, I saw someone who, under different circumstances, might have been a friend. I suddenly realized that Charlie had acted as he had because of the demands and expectations of his own superiors, and the pressures they imposed on him. That didn't justify his aggressive behavior, but it did explain it. Hostility was neither his normal state nor his preferred state. Under it all, he had been suffering.

BEFORE   AFTER

This was an unusual opportunity to get a glimpse of the story behind the story, and it helped me appreciate the extent to which people's behavior may be the result of factors completely external to my interaction with them. I'm now more likely to wonder what could be causing a "difficult" person to act this way than to feel personally offended. I think about what I might be able to do to create a more positive relationship.

Sometimes, of course, it is personal. I'm not going to claim I'll never again take it personally if someone accuses me of incompetence. When Nathan, in Chapter 3, made that accusation, it *was* personal. But when I saw the change in Charlie, I realized that Nathan, his vice president, was under great pressure too, and probably even greater pressure than Charlie had faced. I now look upon people like Charlie and Nathan much differently.

RELATIONSHIP PITFALLS

Yes, even something as positive as building and maintaining strong relationships carries potential pitfalls. One pitfall is that you'll do too much for customers with whom you have strong relationships. When one of my friends became one of my customers, we each put in extensive overtime helping the other meet our respective deadlines. We used to kid about how we'd be better off if we hated each other. Clearly, a strong relationship can create its own workload. It can also lead you to tolerate more lapses from your customers than you might normally, because you don't want to damage your relationship.

Closely related is the pitfall of friendly customers who choose not to complain even when complaints to management would give you the clout you need to request some changes. This situation sometimes occurs when staff shortages and growing workloads cause service quality to slip, but customers fear that reporting declining service will hurt you. It's a little strange to hear yourself asking customers, "*Pleeeeze* complain," so if you're in this situation, your challenge is to help customers not "complain," but make a reasoned business case about how they could benefit if you acquired additional resources.

Another potential pitfall is that you'll do a less than adequate job of meeting the needs of customers with whom you have a strong relationship. You may reject the idea of "wasting" their time with a lot of questions or in-depth analyses, and falsely assume that customers will tell you what you need to know. You may also falsely assume that, given the rapport you have with them, they will know what they need to tell you. Your efforts and your customers' to ease the demands you make on the other could lead to disappointment on both sides.

Of course, just as friends give each other more leeway, both you and your customers may occasionally expect special treatment from the other, thereby putting the other in the uncomfortable position of either turning down a friend, or else feeling obligated to render special favors. Similarly, you may give the arguments of your allies undue credit, while discounting the arguments of your adversaries. Sometimes, a not-quite-so-strong relationship has its benefits.

Do these potential pitfalls suggest that you shouldn't make the effort to develop allies, build rapport, and foster win-win relationships? Not at all. Rather, they simply suggest that any effort, no matter how positive, has a potential downside, and that by being aware of the possibilities you will be better prepared to deal with them if they occur. Even in relationship building—or maybe I should say, especially in relationship building—you must be aware of the impact your actions have on expectations.

Build Relationships with Colleagues

When relationships among systems groups are adversarial or just not as smooth as they might be, the result is growing tension that has a debilitating impact both on the individuals involved and on customers.

This impact can become a critical issue in your ability to manage your customers' expectations of you, because just as systems personnel often view customers as one large homogeneous group, customers often view systems staff similarly. Rarely do customers understand where one systems department ends and the next begins, and when any systems individual delivers poor service or publicly finds fault with other systems staff, it damages the reputation of the entire systems organization.

Therefore, if relationships among systems groups in your organization are not as positive as you believe they should be, use the ideas in this chapter as a starting point to improve the situation: Arrange department-specific gatherings. Hold interdepartmental exchanges. Acknowledge your mistakes. Remember the basic courtesies. Take steps to turn negative relationships into positive ones and to convert adversaries into allies. Above all, try to avoid viewing the problem as someone else's; look inward and think about what you might be doing to perpetuate a less-than-positive relationship. The idea is not to eliminate conflict; that's impossible. In fact, conflict can at times be wholly productive.[2] The idea is to create an environment where you can have win-win relationships not just with customers, but also with each other.

In my experience conducting relationship-building sessions, I have seen something almost magical happen as people step outside their professional role, even briefly, and begin to see each other as human beings. In one such case, for example, I was working with several systems departments that had to interact extensively, but had an adversarial relationship. Part way through the session, during a small-group discussion in which I'd placed two of the strongest adversaries together, I heard one of them say to the other, "You went to college there? So did I."

Suddenly, for the first time, these two individuals saw each other not as adversaries, not as enemies, but as people. And they realized that for all their differences, they had some things—and maybe even many things—in common.

By the end of our session, the entire group had collectively identified what they viewed as their biggest obstacles in working together, and had developed a list of steps they wanted to take to help each other. The steps included identifying problems that cross departmental boundaries, communicating with each other more regularly, presenting a consistent view of their services to customers, and spending time with each other on service calls to better understand the pressures each faces in responding to customers' needs. As the session concluded, several participants said the same thing as the manager in the cross-functional exchange, "We ought to meet like this more often." This type of reversal is not at all unusual when groups take time out from their immediate demands to get to know each other better.

Relationship building among functionally related groups is not a prerequisite to building relationships with customers. But if you think that reducing the level of daily tension among these groups won't help you better meet customers' expectations, just try it and see.

ALL'S WELL THAT MENDS WELL

My tailor didn't need to read this chapter to understand relationships. When I returned to pick up my jacket, he had it waiting for me. "You have good taste in jackets," he told me. "It's a beautiful color." That, I decided to take personally.

NOTES

[1]Stephen Covey describes an experience in meeting with a staff member to confront him about differences in roles, goals, and expectations. He viewed the individual as "such a hard man, so set in his own ways and so right in his own eyes." Covey went through a mental dress rehearsal before the meeting. When they met, he found, to his surprise, that this man "had been going through the very same process and had been longing for such a conversation. He was anything but hard and defensive." Stephen Covey, *The 7 Habits of Highly Effective People* (New York: Simon & Schuster, 1989), pp. 201-202.

[2]In fact, as Peter Senge points out, it's a myth to believe that great teams are characterized by an absence of conflict. He points out that "one of the most reliable indicators of a team that is continually learning is the visible conflict of ideas. In great teams, conflict becomes productive." Peter M. Senge, *The Fifth Discipline: The Art and Practice of the Learning Organization* (New York: Doubleday, 1990), p. 249.

Conclusion:
Formulate an Action Plan
How to be a great expectations manager

When I address large groups on the subject of managing expectations, several listeners invariably comment afterward that it's just common sense. When I hear this comment, I am gratified that these people see the situation as I do. It is common sense, after all, to communicate with care, challenge assumptions, ask questions, and inform customers about changes that will affect them. It's sensible to make sure that you understand what customers want, and that they understand what you can and cannot do for them. It even makes sense to say "I can't help you now" (when appropriate, of course).

But if all these things are common sense, why isn't everyone already doing them? The answer is that even common sense is easy to forget when you're busy trying to squeeze too much work into too little time. That's why occasional reminders are so helpful. After all, just because something is common sense doesn't mean it's second nature. Therein lies your challenge: to make managing expectations second nature to you. If this book has raised your awareness of the role expectations play, and has helped you to generate ideas for improvement, then you're well on your way.

Ideas alone, however, will change nothing. To improve your service effectiveness, you must translate those ideas into action. That's what this final chapter will help you do.

DEVELOP AN ACTION PLAN

Taking action on one or two guidelines or a handful of ideas is a great way to start, even if only on an ad hoc, plan-as-you-go basis. However, if you truly want to make managing expectations second nature, you need a plan to systematically manage expectations, not just for the next customer, the next week, the next project, or the next interaction, but consistently and over the long term. Once you have that plan in place, how you apply it to different services, customers, and circumstances may vary, but that you will apply it will become a given.

The importance of an expectations-managing action plan is not only what it can do to improve your service effectiveness, but also what it communicates to your customers—namely that

- You can't do everything for everyone.

- You are committed to serving customers in a way that comes as close as possible to meeting their needs.

- Everyone benefits from working together to manage expectations.

Plan as a Group

Formulating and implementing an action plan that will bring about major change is not an overnight task,[1] but the following process will get you started. This process involves a group effort entailing considerable discussion and brainstorming, and it takes from two days to a week. Go someplace where you can escape interruptions, distractions, and temptations, preferably off-site. I've been repeatedly impressed—and delighted—by the way ideas and solutions percolate to the surface when groups give themselves the time and space to think, and the opportunity to exchange ideas with each other.

If possible, have a facilitator work with you on such tasks as those described in the following sections. Some organizations select a member of their own group to serve in that role; others invite someone else from inside or outside the organization who has facilitation experience. The facilitator's responsibilities may include such tasks as structuring the session; communicating the objectives and seeing that they are met; leading the discussions; ensuring that all views have a chance to be aired; identifying common themes, related ideas, or overlapping issues; taking notes; and reaching closure relative to the group's objectives.

After holding a planning session, have your notes transcribed immediately, and distribute them to participants. Wait at least a week, and then spend another day discussing the additional ideas that you've generated. In particular, discuss what your observations tell you about your current strengths and weaknesses in managing expectations, and what changes you'd like to make in the way you function.

Assess Your Current Efforts

Begin your planning session with a variation of the three context-setting steps outlined in the Introduction:

Step 1: Discuss your current service strategies.

Step 2: Perform an expectations analysis.

Step 3: Target one or two key problems for resolution.

Conduct these activities as a facilitated group discussion. If your group is large, divide into small groups of three to five each for initial discussions, then hold a full group discussion to compare the views of the smaller groups. These discussions will help you gain a perspective of what's working, what's not, what you'd like to change, and what you'd like to keep the same.

In the course of discussing these issues, be sure to highlight ways in which the group has done well in managing expectations. Most groups have done more than they give themselves credit for; yet recognition for doing so is rare. These discussions will also help to identify similarities and differences in viewpoints. Identifying differences is especially important as it can be difficult to successfully implement an expectations-managing action plan if each participant has different views about the problems under consideration.

In order to give these three steps adequate coverage, try to allocate at least a full day. If you face severe time constraints and find it difficult to get away for lengthy periods as an entire group, concentrate on these three steps, and postpone discussion of what follows until a later time. Most organizations that try this approach find that the insights they gain into their expectations-related problems, and the ideas they generate for addressing them, more than compensate for the time away.

REVIEW THE THREE CENTRAL ISSUES

The three key issues that provide a framework for managing expectations—communication, information gathering, and policies and practices—also provide a framework for evaluating what you must do to improve your expectations-managing ability. Devote part of your planning session to discussing these issues and others that you deem appropriate. The following will help you refocus on these issues. Use the bulleted questions listed for each issue as a basis for discussing your service effectiveness:

1. Communication. Because no two people view the world in exactly the same way, the message a sender sends is not always the one the recipient receives.[2] This is true of people who don't know each other well. It may be even more true of people who do know each other well, because they may be more likely to falsely assume they understand each other. Develop the habit of asking yourself and others,

- How might you be misunderstanding your customers and coworkers?

- In what ways might those you communicate with misinterpret your ideas and advice?

- Can you describe a situation in which you thought you understood what you were told, but later discovered you didn't?

2. Information gathering. You can't meet customers' expectations if you don't know what they want or what's important to them. Yet finding out is not always straightforward. Even when the situation seems simple, it is often fraught with opportunities for misinterpretation. Therefore, you must become an information-gathering skeptic by fine-tuning your information-gathering skills and becoming an expert assumption-checker. And you must educate your customers to do the same.

- What are you doing well in identifying your customers' needs? How do you know you're doing it well?

- What assumptions have you made about customers' problems that caused you to misjudge the problem?

- What can you and your customers do, individually and together, to improve your ability to identify and understand requirements?

3. Policies and practices. No matter how effectively you believe you are serving and supporting your customers, you can't gauge your effectiveness on your own. You must get your customers' perspective. If customer perceptions seem at odds with how you thought you were perceived or how you want to be perceived, examine how you can modify or improve these perceptions. You also need to establish service standards that both you and your customers can reasonably follow. Build and strengthen your relationship with your customers by communicating a win-win mindset and a "we're in this together" orientation.

- What can you do, periodically or continually, to ensure you understand your customers' perceptions of you, and to detect any changes in perceptions before they translate into problems?

- What kinds of service standards would help you better manage your expectations of yourself?

- How can you do more to develop alliances? Once you have done so, how can you use these alliances so that all of you benefit?

CREATE YOUR STRATEGY

With these issues of communication, information gathering, and policies and practices as a guide, examine how the challenges and problems you face may be a consequence of your own performance. Then use the book's twelve guideline-based chapters to formulate a plan of action. The guidelines are reviewed below.

As you work, consider the two suggested action items listed after each guideline. Note that the first action item challenges you to assess your current or recent performance; the second describes either a suggested change or an evaluation you can perform to identify appropriate changes. Using these suggestions, work as a group to create your own list of activities that you will undertake with regard to each guideline.

Guideline #1: Guard against conflicting messages.

- Review your documents and procedures to see if you can identify situations in which you violate your own standards, and think about how doing so may cause unintended expectations.

- Identify changes you can make either in your standards or your adherence to these standards—so that your standards and your actions are in sync with each other.

Guideline #2: Use jargon with care.

- Identify several examples of terminology that you use regularly that might have had different meanings to different individuals or groups.

- Initiate a review of your most widely distributed written material, and make changes to increase clarity and precision.

Guideline #3: Identify communication preferences.

- Review experiences in which you might have been more successful if you had taken your customers' communication preferences into account.

- Analyze the communication preferences of the customers you work with, and determine what steps you might take to work more effectively with them.

Guideline #4: Listen persuasively.

- Think about ways in which you may have given customers the impression you were not listening attentively.

- Analyze each other's listening style and identify changes that might improve the impact you make on customers.

Guideline #5: Help customers describe their needs.

- Analyze an experience in which you might have done better at understanding customer needs if they had something to serve as a focal point for explaining how their requirements were similar or different.

- Identify ways to give customers a chance to say "That's not it"—and as a result, to better express what they want.

Guideline #6: Become an information-gathering skeptic.

- Play "If we knew then what we know now" and identify questions you wish you had asked customers that might have helped you avoid subsequent problems.

- Create a master list of questions to challenge your assumptions and those of your customers.

Guideline #7: Understand your customers' context.

- Review an experience in which you focused too intensively on the immediate situation and didn't adequately gain a perspective of the context.

- Prepare a list of information-gathering questions to guide you in broadening your perspective of factors that affect and are affected by a given problem.

Guideline #8: Try the solution on for size.

- Identify a project in which customers insisted they knew what they wanted and you felt otherwise, and review how you handled the situation.

- Identify two or more methods you can use to help customers "try on" the solution earlier in the project cycle.

Guideline #9: Clarify customer perceptions.

- Analyze the way you communicate your services to your customers, and consider the pluses and minuses of this approach.

- Identify changes you can make that will help customers better understand how you can help them.

Guideline #10: Set uncertainty-managing service standards.

- Review a situation in which effective service standards might have prevented problems from occurring.

- Evaluate the advantages and pitfalls of your department's approach to setting service standards, and consider how you can modify this approach.

Guideline #11: When appropriate, just say whoa.

- Identify ways in which your service strategies may have led customers to expect more than you can reasonably deliver.

- Make a list of situations in which you might appropriately *just say whoa.*

Guideline #12: Build win-win relationships.

- Analyze an experience in which you could have more effectively served a customer if your relationship had been stronger.

- Formulate some ongoing methods for strengthening relationships with your customers, including at least one customer who is often viewed as difficult.

Prepare Your Own To-Do List

Don't panic! You don't have to complete all these activities during your planning session; you simply have to decide which ones you want to include in your plan. When you finish creating your to-do list, first spend two minutes in silence thinking about all the problems that might not have been problems and all the situations that might have run more smoothly if you had already implemented some of the items on your list. Next, convert your list into a specific timetable, along with assignments and accountabilities—and let the implementation begin.

BECOME AN EXPECTATIONS MANAGER

Whether you devote a lot of time to developing an action plan or just a little, whether you go off-site or stay close to the ringing phone, whether you work as a group or individually, I hope you will begin to routinely think about the impact of expectations on all your activities. Doing so will make you an astute expectations manager. However, to ensure that expectations managing stays high up on your to-do list, it may make sense to make expectations management an assigned, and specifically delegated, responsibility. If so, consider appointing someone to structure and oversee efforts from an expectations-managing perspective.

Role Responsibilities

The role of expectations manager can be either a permanent or a rotating responsibility. I favor the latter, so that many people have a chance to "own" the problem and recommend solutions. Alternatively, assign to one member of each work group expectations-managing responsibilities that pertain to that group's efforts. This, too, could be a rotating position, so that each person in the group has the opportunity to develop, recommend, and promote good expectations-managing habits.

Serving as expectations manager is certainly not a full-time responsibility; in fact, it should take only a small portion of time to do the following:

- Help departmental teams consider their services from an expectations-managing perspective, making recommendations to help each group improve its effectiveness.

- Work with teams charged with specific expectations-managing tasks, such as implementing service standards or reviewing existing policy manuals and service guides.

- Review past efforts from an expectations perspective and document this information so the group can benefit from lessons learned.

- Assess the success of expectations-managing efforts and report these successes to the entire group.

- Monitor and report the status of formal expectations-managing efforts, and update the group's overall plan of action.

- Facilitate meetings or other types of information-sharing among the expectations managers from multiple work groups, as well as across departmental lines, to ensure adequate communication on issues that span organizational boundaries. This task would ensure that services are well-integrated from an expectations perspective, and that all relevant parties are appropriately informed of activities that may affect or be affected by their efforts.

The role of expectations manager is not intended to be a fault-finding role. In fact, identifying successes should be explicitly included as a responsibility, both to give credit where appropriate and to apply the learnings from past successes. It's important that expectations managing is viewed as an effectiveness-improving responsibility designed to help everyone do even better.

Personal Action

Whether or not someone is designated as expectations manager, doesn't each individual have a responsibility to manage the expectations associated with his or her own work? In my view,

Absolutely
Positively
YES!

Taking such action is not only important, it's essential. As a minimum, start by saying "Let's be sure we understand what we're each going to do." By doing so, you'll be taking an important step in managing expectations.

Develop the habit of incorporating expectations-managing statements such as the following into your interactions:

- "Let's review what we discussed to make sure we're clear about what we agreed."

- "If I understand correctly, what you expect me to do next is . . ."

- "We'd like to learn more about your upcoming projects so we can plan to be available if you need our help."

- "Could you restate what you're going to do next so I'm sure I didn't overlook anything?"

- "Have I said anything that you'd like me to clarify for you?"

- "My understanding is that, for our next meeting, you will . . . , and I will . . . Is this your understanding also?"

I think of these questions and statements as on-the-fly techniques for managing expectations. They make everyone an expectations manager in his or her own right, independent of any other expectations-managing activities.

Does an awareness of expectations guarantee that others will carry out their end of the bargain? Not at all. But applying expectations-managing techniques will increase the odds that all parties understand what's expected; and that will increase the odds of a successful outcome.

Customer Involvement

Put your efforts into context for your customers by raising the subject of expectations with them. Invite them to work with you to jointly improve the way you manage each other's expectations. Use your ideas from this book as a starting point for a dialogue on the subject. Explain how expectations can contribute to problems, citing problems in the past. You'll find that the very process of talking about expectations will call attention to potentially problematic differences that you may not have recognized otherwise. Indeed, talking about the problem is a major part of the solution.

Remember, though, that the issue of expectations may not be foremost on most people's minds. You, however, have now been thinking about it a lot. Just as you may have initially needed some consciousness-raising on the subject, so may they. Give them time to absorb some of the ideas you've developed. Try to project a "Here's how we all can benefit" attitude.

If you have read this book from the perspective of one who serves customers, go back and review it from the perspective of yourself as the customer. Whichever side of the transaction you're on, you can be instrumental in managing expectations.

START ANYWHERE

How you go about improving your ability to manage expectations is not as important as the fact that you take action. Even small improvements can make a difference. When you finish this book, you can put it on your shelf and get back to work.

Or you can put this book on your shelf, *take some action,* and then get back to work. To make managing expectations successful, keep in mind that it is

- an ongoing responsibility, not a one-time effort.

- something you must do deliberately, conscientiously, and systematically, not as an afterthought.

- something that will not happen if you just sit back and wait for someone else to do it. If it's important to you, you're the one who must make it happen.

Unless you treat expectations management as an ongoing responsibility that you address deliberately, conscientiously, and systematically, then a year from now, nothing will have changed, except possibly for the worse. Remember: If you always do what you've always done, you'll always get what you've always gotten.

Identifying the Predictable

People often react to situations that are predictable as if they were totally unexpected. Clearly, they shouldn't. After all, if something has happened once or twice, there's no excuse for not expecting it. So if you ever hear yourself asking, "Why do they always . . . ?" or "Why don't they ever . . . ?" recognize that you are admitting that the situation was expected. If the situation concerns you, try to understand why it happens, and take steps either to change it or to modify your reaction to it. And, when something happens that you didn't expect, don't let it escape your attention. Reflect on what happened. Success in managing expectations is measured in small steps. Take steps to cause something to continue if you liked it, to prevent a recurrence if you didn't—or, if you have no control over the matter, to be prepared for it the next time it (expectedly) happens. There is really very little that is totally unexpected.

Call Me

Over the years, I've encountered all kinds of situations that revolve around how expectations have been managed. In this book, I've tried to trigger thoughts that will help you better manage expectations in your own work. My Website (www.nkarten.com) features articles and newsletters that offer additional ideas.

If you'd like to discuss your experiences, I'd enjoy hearing from you (781-986-8148 or naomi@nkarten.com). Let's compare our perspectives, share our experiences, and have a few laughs. We can probably both use the break.

NOTES

[1]Stephen Covey describes a situation in which he invited a high-level executive to take six months, along with his staff, to write a corporate mission statement. The executive replied that they'd whip off the statement in a weekend. According to Covey, people frequently seem eager to make major changes, such as changing a company culture, "over a weekend," but he cautions that some things just can't be done so easily or quickly. Stephen R. Covey, *Principle-Centered Leadership* (New York: Simon & Schuster, 1992), p. 16.

[2]For an expanded treatment of this point, see Gerald M. Weinberg, *Quality Software Management, Volume 2: First-Order Measurement* (New York: Dorset House Publishing, 1993), pp. 25-39.

Related Reading

Although this book derives largely from my personal experience and work with client organizations, numerous books have influenced and challenged my thinking. Although you'll find few direct references to expectations in most of these books, every one of them offers valuable insight into the subject.

Albrecht, Karl. *Service Within: Solving the Middle Management Leadership Crisis.* Homewood, Ill.: Dow Jones-Irwin, 1990.

Barker, Joel Arthur. *Paradigms: The Business of Discovering the Future.* New York: HarperCollins, 1993.

Brightman, Harvey J. *Group Problem Solving: An Improved Managerial Approach.* Atlanta: Georgia State University, 1988.

———. *Problem Solving: A Logical and Creative Approach.* Atlanta: Georgia State University, 1980.

Brooks, Frederick P., Jr. *The Mythical Man-Month.* Reading, Mass.: Addison-Wesley Publishing Co., 1975.

Cialdini, Robert B. *Influence: Science and Practice.* Glenview, Ill.: Scott, Foresman and Co., 1985.

Covey, Stephen R. *Principle-Centered Leadership.* New York: Simon & Schuster, 1990.

————. *The 7 Habits of Highly Effective People.* New York: Simon & Schuster, 1989.

de Bono, Edward. *de Bono's Thinking Course.* New York: Facts on File, 1985.

DeMarco, Tom, and Timothy Lister. *Peopleware: Productive Projects and Teams.* New York: Dorset House Publishing, 1987.

Fink, Steven. *Crisis Management: Planning for the Inevitable.* New York: AMACOM, 1986.

Freedman, Daniel P., and Gerald M. Weinberg. *Handbook of Walkthroughs, Inspections, and Technical Reviews: Evaluating Programs, Projects, and Products,* 3rd ed. New York: Dorset House Publishing, 1990.

Gause, Donald C., and Gerald M. Weinberg. *Are Your Lights On? How to Figure Out What the Problem REALLY Is.* New York: Dorset House Publishing, 1990.

————. *Exploring Requirements: Quality Before Design.* New York: Dorset House Publishing, 1989.

Gilovich, Thomas. *How We Know What Isn't So.* New York: The Free Press, 1991.

Hammer, Michael, and James Champy. *Reengineering the Corporation: A Manifesto for Business Revolution.* New York: HarperCollins, 1993.

Karten, Naomi. *Mind Your Business: Strategies for Managing End-User Computing.* Wellesley, Mass.: QED Information Sciences, 1990.

Martel, Myles. *Mastering the Art of Q&A: A Survival Guide for Tough, Trick & Hostile Questions.* Homewood, Ill.: Dow Jones-Irwin, 1989.

Norman, Donald A. *The Design of Everyday Things.* New York: Basic Books, 1988.

Senge, Peter M. *The Fifth Discipline: The Art and Practice of the Learning Organization.* New York: Doubleday, 1990.

van Steenis, Hein. *How to Plan, Develop & Use Information Systems: A Guide to Human Qualities and Productivity.* New York: Dorset House Publishing, 1990.

von Oech, Roger. *A Kick in the Seat of the Pants.* New York: Harper & Row, 1986.

Weinberg, Gerald M. *Quality Software Management, Vol. 2: First-Order Measurement.* New York: Dorset House Publishing, 1993.

———. *Rethinking Systems Analysis & Design.* New York: Dorset House Publishing, 1988.

Wilson, Ralph. *Help! The Art of Computer Technical Support.* Berkeley, Calif.: Peachpit Press, 1991.

Index